WILD RIDE

WILD RIDE

INSIDE UBER'S QUEST FOR WORLD DOMINATION

Adam Lashinsky

PORTFOLIO/PENGUIN

Portfolio/Penguin
An imprint of Penguin Random House LLC
375 Hudson Street
New York, New York 10014
penguin.com

PHOTOGRAPH CREDITS
Insert page 1 (top), 3 (top and bottom), 4 (top), 5 (top): Courtesy of Uber
2 (top): Kevin Smilak
2 (bottom): Courtesy of Francesco Fabbrocino
5 (bottom): Shervin Pishevar
6 (top and bottom), 7 (bottom): Frederique Dame
7 (top): Copyrighted 2017, Mashable, Inc. 127877:0317 AT
8 (top): World Economic Forum
8 (bottom): Angelo Meredino / AFP / Getty Images

Most Portfolio books are available at a discount when purchased in quantity for sales promotions or corporate use. Special editions, which include personalized covers, excerpts, and corporate imprints, can be created when purchased in large quantities. For more information, please call (212) 572-2232 or e-mail specialmarkets@penguinrandomhouse.com. Your local bookstore can also assist with discounted bulk purchases using the Penguin Random House corporate Business-to-Business program. For assistance in locating a participating retailer, e-mail B2B@penguinrandomhouse.com.

LIBRARY OF CONGRESS CATALOGING-IN-PUBLICATION DATA
Names: Lashinsky, Adam, author.
Title: Wild ride : inside Uber's quest for world domination / Adam Lashinsky.
Description: New York : Portfolio, 2017. |
Identifiers: LCCN 2017006832 (print) | LCCN 2017013375 (ebook) |
    ISBN 9780735211407 (ebook) | ISBN 9780735211391 (hardback)
Subjects: LCSH: Uber (Firm) | Ridesharing. | BISAC: BUSINESS & ECONOMICS /
    Corporate & Business History. | BUSINESS & ECONOMICS / Industries /
    Transportation. | BUSINESS & ECONOMICS / Industries / Computer Industry.
Classification: LCC HE5620.R53 (ebook) | LCC HE5620.R53 L37 2017 (print) |
    DDC 388.4/13214—dc23
LC record available at https://lccn.loc.gov/2017006832

Printed in the United States of America
10 9 8 7 6 5 4 3 2 1

Book design by Daniel Lagin

For my family:
Ruth, Leah, Amy, Paula, Robert, Bernard,
and Marcia, whose memory I cherish.

Contents

WILD RIDE

CHAPTER 1

A Wild Ride
Through China

Travis Kalanick sits in the back of a chauffeur-driven black Mercedes making its way through the traffic-clogged streets of Beijing. It is the dead of summer in 2016, and the sky above the Chinese capital is thick with pollution, the air muggy and still. As CEO of Uber, the world's most valuable start-up, Kalanick has been visiting China about every three months for three years now. All the travel from his home base in San Francisco is part of a money-draining and quixotic gambit to replicate the global success of Uber's disruptive ride-hailing service in the world's most populous country.

Kalanick has spent the previous three days in Tianjin, a megacity on the Yellow Sea, two hours southeast of Beijing. There he was a cochair of the World Economic Forum's (WEF) New Champions meeting, the so-called summer Davos. Weeks shy of his fortieth birthday, Kalanick was the toast of Tianjin, where he enjoyed the considerable fringe benefits of his newfound worldwide prominence. The California start-up he runs has been around a mere six years, yet at the off-season international gabfest he scored an audience with the second most powerful government official in China, Premier Li Keqiang. Kalanick appeared on WEF panels moderated by Western and Chinese broadcasters, gamely attempted to flip a traditional pancake over an intimate dinner with the managers responsible for Uber's local operations in Tianjin, and huddled with his entrepreneurial peers. Among them was Lei Jun, founder of the highly valued Chinese smartphone maker Xiaomi. Lei's penchant for bold claims and his company's controversial business model of selling ultracheap phones make him as notorious in China as Kalanick is everywhere else.

Already, Kalanick's trip is a success, judged at least through the prism of the image-enhancing mentions he has racked up in the Chinese and international press. Li, the Chinese premier and an outspoken promoter of entrepreneurialism in China, called Kalanick a "pioneer." He said this in English, a flattering flourish and tidbit the Uber CEO's China-based minions dutifully fed to the local press. Indeed, Kalanick's every utterance on this trip is making headlines. Asked during a WEF fireside chat if self-driving vehicles would make the human-driven kind obsolete, Kalanick threw off one of his signature and controversial one-liners that combined insouciance, boastfulness, and don't-mess-with-me humor. "You might own a car like maybe some people own a horse," he deadpanned in front of an admiring audience. "You know, you might take a ride on the weekends or something."

As he leaves Tianjin and in the privacy of his human-driven vehicle on the road to Beijing, however, his cocky good cheer gives way to prickly tension. In fact, Kalanick has a full-blown crisis on his hands. He joins a conference call with a team of Uber executives in three countries on two continents. A team of communications executives dials in from San Francisco. Others call from Seoul, South Korea. Two executives are in the car with Kalanick, both critical to Uber's Asian ambitions. One is Emil Michael, Uber's chief business officer and the CEO's all-purpose right-hand man, to whom on this very trip Kalanick has delegated the role of engaging in high-stakes and secretive negotiations to sell Uber's China business to its chief rival, Didi Chuxing. The other is Liu Zhen, the head of strategy for Uber China and its best-known Chinese employee. Liu is also a first cousin of Jean Liu, the former Goldman Sachs banker who is president of Didi and whose father founded the computer behemoth Lenovo.

The purpose of the call is to discuss whether or not Kalanick should travel as planned early the next day to Seoul for a most unusual appointment. In late 2014 a Korean prosecutor indicted Kalanick, holding him responsible for what the South Korean government deemed to be Uber's illegal taxi service. This service was a version of the company's popular UberX service in the United States, in which amateur drivers use their own cars to serve passengers. Kalanick agreed to appear in court to answer the charges. The plan, worked out by Uber's legal team after protracted negotiations with the Korean prosecutors, is for Kalanick to plead guilty to what is effectively a misdemeanor—and then to be immediately released.

From a legal perspective, appearing in the Seoul court is low risk. Prosecutors have assured Uber's lawyers that Kalanick would be given a suspended sentence, making him free to leave Seoul. And that would be fine with the CEO, who is well accustomed at this point to picking fights with regulators and other officials the world over. Since it received its first cease-and-desist letter from the city of San Francisco in 2010, Uber has been clashing with adversaries from Seattle to New York and Paris to Delhi and beyond—often with its pugnacious CEO stirring the pot with inflammatory comments to the media and outrageous tweets. What's more, South Korea wasn't all that important a market for Uber, with restrictive laws preventing the company from operating all but the highest-end limousine version of its service there. Uber's motivation in settling the case, therefore, wasn't so much about commerce as about eliminating a pesky and embarrassing thorn in its CEO's side.

As the car snakes its way through snarled Beijing traffic, however, Kalanick becomes increasingly agitated. He's concerned that what ought to be a simple legal proceeding instead has the potential to turn into what he terms a "shit show" on the ground in Korea. Repeatedly, he queries his public-relations and legal advisers about the ramifications of the local media learning that the renegade CEO had alighted in Seoul. The goal was to cause as little ruckus as possible. To achieve that outcome, Uber has chartered a private jet, which stands at the ready at an airfield in Beijing to whisk Kalanick in and out of Korea without the press catching wind of his appearance. And yet someone, likely in the prosecutor's office, has leaked word that Kalanick will appear the next day. Kalanick envisions the worst possible scenario for his and Uber's brand: photos of him being handcuffed and paraded through a Korean courtroom, an Asian perp walk at precisely the moment he was working so hard to project an image of leadership in China and the rest of Asia.

When it comes to protecting his image, no detail is too small. Kalanick wants to know, for example, how many doors there are in the courtroom—the better to understand effective escape routes. How ironclad is the promise to release him immediately? Would he be able to clear customs quietly in the private-aviation terminal? Opinions fly on the line as executives talk over one another, including the CEO. At one particularly heated moment Kalanick instructs his man on the ground in Seoul, Uber's top business-development executive for Asia, to "stop interrupting me."

It will be hours before Kalanick decides to skip the court date and instead instruct his Korean lawyers to request, for the fourth time, an extension. It is a calculated risk. Angering a Korean judge might make Kalanick permanently unwelcome in Korea. And yet the bet pays off, at least in the short term. His failure to appear earns brief mentions in the Korean press and is ignored everywhere else, including in the United States. Months later there is no movement in the case, and there isn't likely to be until Uber decides having a business in Korea is worth the renewed effort.

In the meantime, the Uber entourage reaches its Beijing destination, the glittering Shangri-La Hotel. Next to the hotel is a convention center where Kalanick will address a conference hosted by the Chinese Internet company NetEase. Kalanick and his colleagues briefly hole up in a private room to complete their call as a crowd of one thousand overwhelmingly youthful employees of Chinese Internet companies waits in a strobe-lit hall with loudspeakers blaring.

Despite Uber's underdog status in China, Kalanick is a rock

star to the young, Internet-savvy Chinese audience. Obsessed with all things digital and entrepreneurial, the tech workers know well the story of Uber's global success and its efforts in China. Even though Didi outshines it at home, Uber has carved out a sizable piece of the market, and Kalanick is a boldface name for the audience. The packed ballroom is skeptical but intrigued by Kalanick's maverick reputation and record of persistence. They have no idea how close Uber is to capitulating in China. They also know nothing of how distracted Kalanick is by the prospect of possible arrest in Seoul. The air of excitement in the room is palpable.

For Kalanick, however, it's just another speech, followed by an onstage interview with a local broadcaster with impeccable English. As the attendees don headphones for simultaneous translation, the Uber CEO strides onstage in the crisp gray suit and collared white shirt he'd worn that morning to meet the premier of China. He gives an abbreviated version of a talk he'd delivered months earlier at the world-famous TED conference in Vancouver, including a photo of the Los Angeles suburb where he grew up. This iteration of the talk, though, is tailored for the Chinese audience. Newly added is an update on Uber's three-year-old China business, which by now includes service in some sixty cities. In a brief Q&A following his talk, Kalanick is asked if he minds being second place in the Chinese market, given Uber's leading position most everywhere else in the world. He chuckles and gives a nonanswer: "The way I like to think of this is, it's our job to serve drivers and riders better. If we ultimately serve them better we will have most of the customers. And we still have some work to do." Asked directly about first-place Didi, Kalanick deflects: "In an ideal world we are serving those customers better and most of those customers are ours."

It's late afternoon and not only is Kalanick spent, he has bigger things on his mind than convincing China's Internet community that Uber can best Didi. The appearance lasts barely twenty minutes, after which the CEO hustles out of the hall and to a nearby hotel to mull his Korean dilemma.

By breakfast the next day at the sturdy and sumptuous Rosewood Beijing hotel, the tense pall hanging over Kalanick the day before has lifted completely. Having already decided to skip the Seoul jaunt, Kalanick has moved on. Freshly shaved and dressed in his more typical jeans and a polo shirt, he is rested and relaxed. He professes to be completely over the ordeal and unaffected by it. The back-and-forth with authorities is a necessary dance, he tells me, and he is dutifully executing his steps. In Kalanick's worldview, Uber's entire business model is predicated on challenging obsolete laws meant to protect entrenched interests and frustrate innovation rather than benefit consumers. The whole notion of taxi medallions and fixed pricing, for example, constricts supply and keeps prices high—both negatives for riders. For him, it has become part of the job to fight what he sees as injustice. Where the world sees a provocateur, Kalanick looks in the mirror and sees a truth seeker.

Given that he'd been planning on stealthily jetting to Korea on this fine summer morning, Kalanick has a rare open schedule in front of him; he isn't due in his next destination, Hangzhou, until the next day. After polishing off an omelet he plans to sit at his computer and see "what shit I can stir up," he declares.

And so, at right that moment, Kalanick begins telling me his life story. For the better part of two years I had been attempting to persuade the reluctant CEO to cooperate with me on a book about Uber. As a writer for *Fortune* based in San Francisco, I had been covering Silicon Valley's top companies for nearly twenty years and had written a book about Apple in 2012. After fits and starts and discussions about having further discussions, he had finally relented. I was planning to write the book with or without him, and he made a pragmatic decision to have his say rather than remain quiet. Weeks earlier, he had invited me to tag along on this trip to China, given how central the country was to Uber's story. Kalanick and his advisers also correctly foresaw that a trip far from headquarters would afford moments like this, where the harried executive would have time to talk with me.

Indeed, once Kalanick got to talking, he didn't let up. We continue the conversation over the course of the next several days in China and then again once we'd both returned home to San Francisco. We talk on a flight—on the plane that was supposed to ferry him to Korea—to the coastal city of Hangzhou, where he'll meet with Uber China's top executives as well as Jack Ma, founder of Alibaba and China's Internet kingpin; in a van shuttling him to a resort hotel on the outskirts of Hangzhou; in mid-July back home, during a three-hour walk through the streets of San Francisco; and during numerous additional formal and informal chats after that.

Uber's story isn't strictly synonymous with Travis Kalanick's, but he is its central character. In fact, Uber wasn't initially his idea. Kalanick's involvement with Uber was part time for the entire first year of the company's existence, a time when he was recuperating from his last gig and keeping his options open for his next one. All the same, Kalanick was present nearly at the creation of Uber, and he supplied the critical insight that transformed someone else's idea from merely interesting to undeniably groundbreaking. He has been Uber's iron-fisted, omnipresent CEO from the time it first gained traction and began expanding beyond San Francisco. As a result, Uber has become as identified with Kalanick as Microsoft, Apple, and Facebook are with Bill Gates, Steve Jobs, and Mark Zuckerberg, respectively.

Whether or not Uber becomes as powerful and highly valued as these enduring technology-industry titans, its CEO already has become an object of fascination and, for many, repulsion. In the short period that Uber went from an idea to the biggest of the so-called unicorns—privately held start-ups valued at more than $1 billion, once a rarity—Kalanick became world famous for his ruthlessness, lack of empathy, and willingness to flout anybody else's rules. He was a veritable poster boy for the "brogrammer" culture of San Francisco, a male-dominated universe of engineers-turned-entrepreneurs. Older than Gates, Jobs, and Zuckerberg were when they founded their companies, he arrived on the scene already a B-level fixture in San Francisco's post-Internet-bubble start-up community.

And while Kalanick had struggled with his previous start-ups, his timing with Uber was impeccable. Just as Microsoft defined the personal computer revolution, Apple wrote the next chapter of digital entertainment, and Facebook created the twenty-first century's most powerful publishing platform, Uber perfectly exemplifies all the attributes of the information-technology industry's next wave. A mobile-first company, if there had been no iPhone there would have been no Uber. Uber expanded globally almost from its beginning, far earlier than would have been possible in an era when packaged software and clunky computers were the norm. It is a leader of the so-called gig economy, cleverly marrying its technology with other people's assets (their cars) as well as their labor, paying them independent-contractor fees but not costlier employee benefits. Such "platform" companies became all the rage as Uber rose to prominence. Airbnb didn't need to own homes to make a profit renting them. Thumbtack and Task-Rabbit are just two companies that matched people looking for project-based work with customers—without having to make any hires themselves.

By late 2016 Uber stood at a crossroads. It had raised $17 billion from private investors, reaching a valuation of $69 billion, an unheard-of level for a still-fledgling private company. Within weeks of Kalanick's wild ride through the streets of Beijing, Uber would shock its critics and admirers alike by quitting in China, the country into which Kalanick personally had poured so much energy and credibility, to say nothing of his investors' capital. For nearly twenty years, Kalanick had been the perennial never-say-die entrepreneur. Yet here he was, waving the white flag in China and citing pragmatism as the reason. "As an entrepreneur, I've learned that being successful is about listening to your head as well as following your heart," he said in a blog post announcing the sale of Uber China to Didi.

The odds had been long, yet Uber had appeared to be making

headway in China. If nothing else it had succeeded simply in winning the Chinese government's tacit permission to operate, a feat Google, Facebook, eBay, and others hadn't managed to pull off. Still, Uber was losing a billion dollars a year in China, and by selling to Didi—making Uber Didi's largest shareholder and bringing Didi onto Uber's board—Kalanick in one fell swoop suffered the most painful failure of his career and achieved one of his greatest triumphs. All of a sudden he had turned a $2 billion investment into a stake in a rising Chinese monopoly worth $6 billion. And by eliminating a no-end-in-sight drain on the company's cash reserves, he shored up Uber's finances, paving the way for an eventual initial public offering of Uber's shares in the United States.

Kalanick too stood at a crossroads. From the age of twenty he'd reveled in being the scrappy, rough-edged, loose-lipped entrepreneur. He mightily swung for the fences with the first start-up he was a part of—and lost. His second tech company was a modest, if exhausting, success. With Uber he'd already enjoyed dizzying heights, but at a price. He was known throughout the world as an asshole, a ruthless, authority-defying libertarian, admired for his tenacity but reviled for his scorched-earth tactics. That image didn't sit well with him. Travis Kalanick, even close followers of the Silicon Valley scene might be surprised to know, felt misunderstood.

What wasn't disputable, however, was that he was now the CEO of a large organization, one with annual revenues of about $6 billion and around ten thousand employees. Even he understood that his days of cobbling together a smartphone app and letting the public try it or speaking his mind without consequences were over. An entrepreneur more accustomed to "jamming" on a "hack" to solve a problem consumers didn't know they had, he was now at the epicenter of the business establishment. (In late 2016, then president-elect Donald Trump named Kalanick to an eighteen-member "Strategic and Policy Forum," a group of business advisers. Kalanick hastily resigned the position days after Trump's inauguration amidst outrage by employees and customers over Trump's sudden travel ban on citizens from seven predominantly Muslim countries.) Kalanick's story—and his company's—offers a window into all the most important trends in business in an era defined by smartphones, easy access to capital, and the harnessing of artificial intelligence that computer scientists had dreamed of for years. This book aims to tell the story of this era-defining company and its singular CEO. While it may be impossible to bridge the asshole-versus-misunderstood divide, it is possible to explain how Kalanick and Uber came to be who and what they are—and how they reached such a high pinnacle of success.

I first met Travis Kalanick in July 2011, less than a year after he'd become CEO of Uber. The company was tiny then, with just several hundred licensed limousine drivers using its app, all in San Francisco. Even then, though, Uber had achieved the sheen of a San Francisco start-up on the rise. But Uber was still two years away from adopting the strategy of one of its competitors to allow ordinary people to use their own cars to make money via Uber's app. So while Uber already was cool and buzzy, it hadn't yet gone through the explosive growth that would make it the most highly valued start-up in the world.

At that meeting Kalanick, then thirty-four years old, laid out the basics of his career. A native of Los Angeles, he'd been a computer engineering major who'd dropped out of UCLA to work for a company called Scour, begun by some of his classmates. Scour was a proto-Napster that the entertainment industry shortly sued out of existence. He parlayed the file-sharing concepts of Scour to start another company, Red Swoosh, with the idea of turning "litigants into customers" by building peer-to-peer software for entertainment companies to use for legitimate purposes. Six long years later he sold that company to Akamai, the dominant software competitor in its field, for just enough money for Kalanick to join the club of San Francisco entrepreneurs who had achieved an "exit," a financing event that put some cash in his pocket.

During our first chat Kalanick also told me how Uber got started. It was an after-the-fact creation myth, which nearly every successful Silicon Valley start-up has, about how he and a friend named Garrett Camp had an epiphany when they couldn't catch a cab during a blizzard in Paris in late 2008. If only there were a way to turn one's phone into a taxi dispatcher. "The germ of the idea was Garrett's," Kalanick said. "Mine was the business architecture."

Three years later, Uber was already beloved by its young, largely male customer base—people like Kalanick and Camp who are thrilled with the transformative power of pushing a button on their smartphones and having a Lincoln Town Car show up at their doorstep. Given how contentious Uber's relationship with its drivers would one day become, Kalanick on that day in mid-2011 chose to emphasize how much he loved Uber's drivers. He said he gave them hugs whenever they visited Uber. "When they come here"—to Uber's modest offices at Fourth and Market streets in San Francisco—"I say, 'Let's hug it out.'" He recounted the tale of the company's first crisis, the day the previous fall when the city of San Francisco served Uber a cease-and-desist letter. The company, then named UberCab, decided the city had no jurisdiction over it, first because it was merely a technology platform that owned no cars and employed no drivers, and also because its "partners" drove limos, not taxis. "So we removed the 'Cab' from our name," said Kalanick, and Uber otherwise ignored the city's demand to stop arranging rides.

Kalanick was full of confidence in that summer of 2011. Uber already operated in New York and planned to launch shortly in Seattle, Washington, D.C., Boston, and Chicago. Kalanick bragged about the advanced math that went into Uber's calculation of when riders should expect their cars to show up. Uber's "math department," as he called it, included a computational statistician, a rocket scientist, and a nuclear physicist. They were running, he informed me, a Gaussian process emulation—a fancy statistical model—to improve on data available from Google's mapping products. "Our estimates are far superior to Google's," Kalanick said.

I was witnessing for the first time the cocksure Kalanick. I told him I had an idea for a market for Uber. I had recently sent a babysitter home in an Uber, a wonderful convenience because I could pay with my credit card from Uber's app and then monitor the car's progress on my phone to make sure the sitter got home safely. And I didn't have to leave home to do it. I was certain other parents would want to do the same and that Uber could enhance its image by marketing itself to them. Kalanick could have smiled away the idea. Instead, he made it clear he wasn't interested. My idea didn't conform to Kalanick's image of Uber, a "baller" service that allowed well-heeled single men like him to travel around town in high style. Uber's motto at the time was "Everyone's Private Driver." A service for parents to shuttle home their babysitters? Lame.

Over time, I saw Kalanick out and about in San Francisco, sometimes at the Battery, the tech community's slick private dining club in a converted pre-earthquake marble mill, or at industry conferences. When I told him in a breakfast buffet line that I loved Uber but didn't want or need to be driven around in a luxury car, he told me to be patient, that a new service called UberX would change my mind about Uber.

And by the time Uber became a global phenomenon, I told Kalanick, by e-mail in early 2014, that I wanted to write a book about the company. His response was swift—and in character. "I am a fan of your work, and am flattered that you would consider writing a book about Uber," he wrote. "However, in my opinion it is not the time to do it. I'm not sure if you're planning to write the book anyways, but I will make it clear to the folks I know not to cooperate and if you are still persistent, I will find another writer to write an authorized book with full access to us to compete with yours. It's not my preference to take this approach, but it is an important topic that I feel strongly about." He ended by writing, "Thanks. T."

I felt like I was off to a good start, at least in terms of seeing the real Kalanick. He didn't respond, as many CEOs would have, with some kind of diplomatic answer about perhaps beginning a dialogue we could finish when the timing was better. He flat-out threatened to bury my project if I had the temerity to defy him.

I kept in touch with Kalanick, and eventually he changed his mind about cooperating with me. As Uber got bigger its reputation became more checkered, especially as various missteps caused many riders and drivers to sour on the company. Well-funded competitors also sprang up everywhere Uber did business. These included Lyft and Juno in the United States, Gett in Europe, Didi in China, GrabTaxi in Southeast Asia, and Ola in India. All raised ample funding, sometimes from the same investors that backed Uber. Kalanick and the seasoned advisers he hired gradually came to see that his pugnaciousness has poisoned the well with too many constituencies: investors, government officials, drivers, potential and existing customers. It was not at all uncommon for people in U.S. cities, for example, to refuse to use Uber, citing the company's reputation for rough tactics and attitude toward women. Kalanick would ultimately decide to tell me his story, but on my terms, not his. I would have access to him and Uber's other executives, but the story would be mine alone to tell.

Like any company, Uber remains a work in progress. But mere years into its existence it had so insinuated itself into the cultural zeitgeist that it joined an elite group of corporate names that double as verbs: *No need to drive to the event, I'll just Uber there.*

Consumers took to Uber so quickly because it is so easy to use. Each time the company opens for business in a new market—at the end of 2016 it operated in more than 450 cities in 73 countries—users discuss their discovery with the zealousness of a convert. Unlike naysayers of Twitter, who try the service but can't see the utility, or doubters of Snapchat, who believe, justifiably, they're too old to learn, Uber appeals to everyone who lives in or near a city and has a smartphone. A new customer installs the app, enters their credit card information (personal and business, if they choose), and then requests a driver. The software knows where the request is coming from because the customer's smartphone has a GPS chip (and other sensor technology) that tells it so. Uber uses the same technology to know where the closest driver is. Customers quickly adapt to simply exiting an Uber car without paying because Uber automatically charges their card and pays the driver their cut. What is now commonplace for many was magical the first time they did it—and a massive departure from fumbling for cash or persuading a cabbie to take plastic in days gone by.

Though it began by catering to urban, on-the-prowl hipsters with plenty of disposable income, Uber knows few demographic boundaries. It appeals to single women who can get a safe, trackable ride home. Senior citizens can use the service as easily as teenagers. UberPool, a carpooling service, makes Uber affordable to anyone with just a little more cash than bus fare. The company even reasonably argues that its service has become a social good. It is an antidote to drunk driving, for instance. Uber cleverly tapped into the national angst over unemployed military veterans by designing a program to recruit vets as drivers. More than fifty thousand signed up.

Uber unleashed the promise of other societal shifts. It replaced the antiquated taxi radio dispatch system, for example, with an algorithmic rider request/driver availability matching program. Some taxi services built apps of their own in response. Where the company has sufficient scale, in all its major cities, the system is so efficient that power users have begun to think the unthinkable: car ownership isn't so necessary anymore. As well, Uber's carpooling aspirations portend to eliminate congestion itself. If people don't own cars and ride in them with other people more, at least in theory there would be fewer cars on the street. Should the vision of autonomous vehicles become a reality—and Uber is investing heavily in the technology—roads may become less crowded for the first time since the invention of roads.

That said, it's easy to get carried away with Uber's promise— and Uber frequently does. Car ownership hasn't yet declined in the United States as the result of the advent of ridesharing or for any other reason. According to U.S. Census data, the percentage of households with no vehicles declined from 21.5 percent in 1960 to 9.1 percent in 2010, the year Uber started. It was the same four years later, the last data available. There is similar national data for driver's licenses: The number ticked up by four million from 2014 to 2015, also according to census data. As well, the Pew Research Center reported in 2016 that while 51 percent of Americans had heard of the concept of ridesharing, just 15 percent had used a service like Uber and Lyft, and another 33 percent were unfamiliar with them altogether. Surveys suggest that Uber has had a meaningful impact on the life of young adults in urban areas but hasn't yet triggered the kind of societal change it frequently trumpets.

Uber does represent a new opportunity for drivers, if a challenging one. Becoming an Uber driver is easy. (To prove the point, I got behind the wheel while researching this book.) And it offers the ultimate labor flexibility. Want to make a little extra cash when you have the time to do it? Just open the app and wait for your first request. At a time of economic anxiety, Uber extends a lifeline to those trying to make ends meet. At the same time, Uber has relentlessly lowered prices in order to lock in its relationship with riders. The result is a constant churn of drivers, necessitating an endless loop of recruitment of replacements. Driving on the Uber platform may be a great way to earn beer money. But it's a tough way to earn a full-time living.

The dark side of Uber's rise is ample too. There's something a little scary about getting into a car with a total stranger, though an Uber ride, unlike a trip in a taxi, can be tracked. The story of Uber is an endless series of on-the-one-hand/on-the-other-hand conundrums: the ability to track trips is comforting but brings with it the nefarious potential for digital stalking. Consider: passengers who input their home address into the Uber app are indicating, at least to Uber, where they live. Indeed, every time an Uber driver is accused of rape, global headlines follow. Early in its existence Uber adopted a technique called surge pricing intended to get more drivers on the road. Rational to someone with a solid grasp of the laws of supply and demand—scarcity boosts prices, which then gooses supply—the move infuriated and alienated customers facing surging prices, especially during snowstorms and other natural disasters. (It didn't help when Kalanick basically told Uber customers to quit their whining.) Indeed, as Uber grew from phenomenon to an established business, its every move courted controversy. Its maverick reputation quickly gave way to the perception of a company that considered itself above the law. Drivers traveled a relatively short path from loving Uber for the cash it put in their pockets to complaining that Uber was paying them less and denying them the full benefits of employment. (Nearly 400,000 drivers in California and Massachusetts joined a class-action suit against Uber, which Uber agreed to settle for $100 million. A federal judge later rejected the settlement, delaying a resolution of the dispute.) All this happened in the span of roughly two years, beginning in the middle of 2013, when UberX first took off.

⦿————————————————————————————⦿

At the center of this story, of course, is Travis Kalanick, who came to define what it meant to be a tech entrepreneur in the second decade of the twenty-first century. Kalanick is different from the last class of Silicon Valley billionaire sensations, and Uber is a different tech company. Google, Facebook, Twitter, and others were pure "Internet" companies. Their products existed in digital formats only. From its beginning Uber was an Internet technology company that coexisted with physical objects, namely automobiles. Running it required someone who could master the new science of computers and the older arts of the industrial economy, including logistics.

Uber and its CEO forced even successful investors to think differently about how the landscape was changing. "Investment is all about pattern recognition," says Yuri Milner, the Russian physicist-turned-investor who put $200 million into Facebook when it was a young company, a bet that returned billions. "It turns out Uber was a different pattern. I felt most of the pure Internet businesses already had been invented when Uber started. The paradigm was coders working for several years in isolation, with no interaction with the physical world or government agencies or the public. Then a new business model arose. It was offline plus online. That called for a different kind of founder. It called for someone who can interact with the outside world. Travis is a fighter. It's totally different."

Kalanick would come to develop an alternative lingo to explain Uber's contradictory impulses. He called it "bits and atoms," the critical combining of software with the material world. He personally embodied the combination: a math nerd who ran track in high school, the geek who could hang with the cool kids, a computer engineer with the gift of gab.

For Kalanick, Uber also was the culmination of his experiences to date as an entrepreneur, the sum total of his failures and successes—plus the usual right-time/right-place luck. Paul Sagan, who as CEO of Akamai bought Kalanick's company Red Swoosh, has observed Uber's CEO from a distance for years. He calls Kalanick "the Goldilocks of Silicon Valley entrepreneurs." His first company, Scour, Sagan said, was too hard—a shooting star that flamed out spectacularly. Red Swoosh was too soft—a labor of love for Kalanick that was never going to be a business. "Uber," says Sagan, "is just right."

"Just right" is understatement, of course. Silicon Valley is packed with strivers, dreamers, and mercenaries certain they will change the world, realize untold riches, and etch their names on virtual monuments to the power of innovation and disruption.

Almost none of these entrepreneurs will succeed. The cynical venture capitalists who fund them know this: VCs can consider their funds fantastic successes if one in ten of their investments pays off. This means they are resigned to the other nine being failures.

Uber, then, no matter what happens next, already has defied these odds. It has built a substantial, global, sometimes profitable business that has wreaked havoc on incumbent players from taxi companies to rental-car agencies. Operating from a playbook he devised more or less himself, Travis Kalanick also has defied the odds. A college dropout like Steve Jobs, Bill Gates, and Mark Zuckerberg before him, unlike them he knew failure first and then only modest success. He burst onto the world stage more fully formed than those gawky youths, yet his edges were every bit as rough, his ambition possibly greater. As with all success stories, Kalanick's path was anything but linear, and Uber's continued dominance of its chosen markets is anything but guaranteed. Indeed, in the first months of 2017, Kalanick faced a new crisis very nearly every day: complaints of rampant sexism in Uber's engineering ranks, a video of him berating a longtime Uber driver, a lawsuit alleging fraud by Google's self-driving car unit, the revelation that Uber used software tricks to elude law-enforcement officials where it operated illegally.

For all that, Uber's story remains a tale of our times: of the transformative power of technology, the impermanence of long-term employment, and the opportunity in Silicon Valley and virtual communities like it to turn scrappiness, moxie, and smarts into vast fortunes.

CHAPTER 2
Training Wheels

I n the mid-1990s, the sun-speckled campus of the University of California, Los Angeles, in LA's Westwood neighborhood, was known for many things. The Bruins of football and basketball fame were perennial contenders. UCLA boasted a first-rate film school, conveniently located in Hollywood's backyard. Its medical center was world class, not least because of the multitude of Southern California's rich and famous in its care. What UCLA was not, however, was a hotbed for start-up companies founded by computer nerds. The center of gravity for computer science is 350 miles north, in Silicon Valley, its epicenter on the campus of Stanford University in Palo Alto. Stanford alumni Jerry Yang and David Filo had already started Yahoo, a wildly popular compilation of searchable Web pages. Larry Page and Sergey Brin were Stanford graduate students fiddling with an algorithm that would soon become Google. The world's leading venture capitalists, investors who make risky bets on unproven technology companies, nearly all had their offices on Sand Hill Road in Menlo Park, min-utes from the Stanford campus. The proximity was no coinci-dence: the financiers recognized the value of staying close to the people dreaming up investable ideas at Stanford's venerable com-puter science and engineering schools.

This isn't to say UCLA's programs were an engineering back-water. For decades the university had pumped out rocket scien-tists and other engineers to serve the defense and aerospace industries that had grown up nearby after World War II. And it laid claim to its own piece of computer history. In 1969, computer scientists working out of a room in Boelter Hall, the school's engi-neering building, sent the very first message over a government-funded communications network called the ARPANET. From that first transmission between two "nodes" on the network—the receiving node, as it happened, was at Stanford—the Internet was born.

Twenty-five years later that history would have been merely a gauzy tale of yesteryear for UCLA's undergraduate computer students, even as the latest evolution of the Internet, the World Wide Web, was spawning a multitude of lucrative businesses. What young software coders on campus did know was that they enjoyed one another's unique company and that it was good to have a place to hang out together. That place at UCLA, also in Boelter Hall, was the school's Undergraduate Computer Science Association (UCSA). It was, says Michael Todd, an association member in the mid-1990s, a kind of "clubhouse," a place like-minded students could relax together after class while they played games and talked computers. The club also served as a "résumé builder," Todd recalls, a signal to future employers that hardware and software were an important part of a young job seeker's life.

With its storage-room collection of computer equipment and mismatched couches, the association functioned as something of a fraternity, a vibe reinforced by the scarcity of young women. Friendships formed quickly among the undergrads. Ilya Haykinson, whose family had emigrated from Moscow when he was a child, was friends with Todd, who hailed from Marin County, a comfy suburb north of San Francisco. An introvert, Haykinson recalls happily falling in with the crowd at the UCSA. A classmate named Dan Rodrigues was president of the club for a time. Two other members were Vince Busam, an avid volleyball player who lived in the same dorm as Todd, and Kevin Smilak, another Bay Area native.

The student destined to become the club's most famous member grew up practically next door. Travis Kalanick, who came from the nearby San Fernando Valley and was pursuing a double major in computers and business, quickly gravitated toward the club. He remembers finding more kinship among its members than residents of his dorm. "I spent most of my time there," he recalls. "We would play Double Dragon," a popular "beat-'em-up" video game from the 1980s that by then had migrated from video arcades to personal computers. The servers at the computer club, which belonged to the school's computer science department, allowed members to exploit a networking technique called file transfer protocol, or FTP, to search for programs located elsewhere on the Internet. Kalanick remembers: "We would find FTP sites with MP3s"—files that digitally compressed music to be stored on a computer—"and we would do these weird puzzles and brain teasers. That's what we did."

Despite the boom in Internet companies up north, the computer club was mostly about fun and games. It was in that vein that Busam had an idea in the fall of 1997. At the time, all the Windows-based computers in the UCLA dorms, that is, those that used Microsoft software as their operating system, were networked to one another. Shockingly, at least by later standards, the default setting on those computers allowed them not only to communicate with one another but for the files stored on them to be shared among all users on the network without a password. "There was no such thing as firewalls," says Kalanick.

Such laxity created an opportunity. Busam got it in his head that it'd be fun to create a program that would automatically search for music and other so-called multimedia files on all the connected computers and then index the results. The technique already was familiar to anyone who used Internet search engines to "crawl" the Web looking for information or entertainment sites. The original intent was simply to digitally replicate the time-honored practice of college kids lending out their albums around the floor. "We started this in Vince's dorm room to find music and listen to it," says Todd, who helped Busam write the initial code.

The duo may have been operating out of a college dormitory, but thanks to the magic of networking—something that would not have been possible before that first ARPANET transmission from Boelter Hall—they had access to UCLA's massive computers. Todd was a systems administrator, a part-time position that gave him a "key" to the network. He and Busam realized that their program that could find songs throughout the dorm would work just as well in other dorms and even on other campuses. It worked, in fact, with any computer connected to the Internet, meaning that if they could build and publicize such a service, there might even be a business to be built by amassing a large audience of computer-savvy music lovers. Some of their computer club buddies caught wind of their "hack," and by November 1997 Smilak, Rodrigues, and a fifth classmate, Jason Droege, joined Todd and Busam to see if they could make a company of the music-file crawling idea. (Kalanick, away that term in Portland, Oregon, on an internship with semiconductor giant Intel, wasn't part of the original crew.) The group had little business experience, but they did have a knack for naming a new company. They came up with Scour, a catchy name for a tool that would scrub a network's files looking for MP3s—and eventually videos too.

At first, though, what became Scour.net was more of a student project than a company. During winter break the group got together to beef up the code. They holed up in Walnut Creek, California, at Smilak's parents' home near San Francisco, where they placed their computers on a ping-pong table in a guesthouse near the pool. (Smilak's stepfather, James Umphreys, would become Scour's first investor, putting in several thousand dollars. A friend of Dan Rodrigues's father also invested.) Initially, the Scour team spent next to nothing to start the company. Back at UCLA for the next term, at the beginning of 1998, they created a Web site that essentially was UCLA property because it ran on the university's network and had a campus Web address: scour.cs.ucla.edu. They also slightly expanded the core group, adding Haykinson early in the year.

The student who eventually would become the seventh member of the founding group, Kalanick, hadn't been around when things got going due to his internship at Intel. He was already tight with the group of friends who started Scour, though, especially Rodrigues, who also had planned to join Kalanick that fall at Intel but changed his mind and stayed in Los Angeles instead. Kalanick feared he was missing out—and let Rodrigues know it. "I was miffed a little bit, and I was like, 'Really, dude? I want to be in the game,'" remembers Kalanick. He didn't sign on with Scour in earnest until later in the school year because he had another internship that summer, this time working on an electricity-industry project in Los Angeles with Boston Consulting Group. It was not the last time Kalanick would hang back from a fledgling start-up while he considered his options; he would do it again a decade later as Uber took flight.

Scour was a perfect example of what would later be described as an ideal product-market fit, an almost totemic term among Silicon Valley entrepreneurs. Some start-ups make a nifty product that nobody wants. Others go after a massive market but have nothing to offer. Scour was a simple-to-use Web site that identified and listed music files available on a network, which greatly appealed to a market of college students who wanted to discover new music but could afford to buy only so many CDs. Scour's promise was to build a large audience that would be commercially attractive to entertainment companies, either as a promotional vehicle or as a sales platform. Scour didn't own the key assets that attracted its users, songs its users had purchased. Rather, it was an early example of a "platform" that leveraged other people's property for its own commercial gain. What Scour's users' music files were to Scour, UberX's drivers' cars would become to Uber, though Uber would fare far better than Scour.

Word spread quickly about Scour's service, now an official business. "We were literally in our dorms just watching this thing grow on a daily basis," says Droege, a computer major who had taken courses at UCLA's film school and had a sense of the company's potential as a media business. "Something like eleven percent of the students at Berkeley were Scour users within like six months of launch. It was this very college kiddy thing, and the IT dorm police never noticed that the server was there, even though we were proxying like twenty megabits a second of traffic. Back then, that much bandwidth would cost you like twenty thousand dollars a month to buy."

Scour grew so quickly, in fact, that its founders faced a difficult choice: education or entrepreneurialism. "It's difficult sitting in physics class, when not a lot of people have cell phones, and have your phone buzzing continuously because your servers in San Jose are down," says Haykinson. "Eventually that got to be too much. A number of us withdrew from classes." A division of labor that happened organically solidified toward the end of 1998. Rodrigues, later Scour's president, was the business guy and was fond of applying lessons learned from the many business books he read. Smilak and Busam wrote software. Todd managed the servers. Droege ran advertising, initially selling banner ads. By the time the group moved out of the UCLA dorm and into a Westwood apartment rented by Todd and Rodrigues, Kalanick, who also stopped going to class, had joined the team and handled marketing as well as a task that would prove critical throughout his career: fund-raising. He was, in effect, knowledgeable about the technology but never the primary coder, a business role he'd stick with for years.

By early 1999 Scour was beginning to resemble a company, albeit one run by a bunch of college dropouts working from a cramped apartment next to their erstwhile university. "We got to thirteen people working in an office with as many computers," says Haykinson, who years later would become director of engineering for the messaging service Snapchat, located across town in Venice. "Whenever anyone used the microwave we'd have to turn the power off on the monitors so it didn't blow the fuses. It was sort of ridiculous."

The Scour team's origins as entrepreneurial renegades, whether it was appropriating UCLA's network or building a business off intellectual property they didn't own, made an imprint on the company—and its founders. "One of the things we learned was that we would do these little innocuous, kind of quirky things and nobody would really penalize us," says Droege, the only member of the core Scour group who eventually would join Kalanick at Uber, the ultimate maverick technology company. "We kind of realized how you can bend the rules, as long as you're doing something that doesn't necessarily hurt anybody. But you're using these systems to your advantage. And so we just tried to go a little bit deeper each time."

To go as deep as it wanted, Scour needed to raise more money, and the founders soon aimed beyond friends and family. Smilak's stepfather had invested an additional $150,000, but it wasn't sufficient to pay themselves and to rent server space. (Running on UCLA's network was no longer an option.) Todd was friends with a former UCLA computer science graduate student named Francesco Fabbrocino, who would later be his roommate. Fabbrocino worked at an Internet start-up in Beverly Hills called Checkout.com, which was controlled by the Hollywood agent Michael Ovitz and Ron Burkle, who had made his billions in supermarkets. Like many others in this era, they were keen on cashing in on the Internet craze. On the assumption that they might be interested in investing in Scour too, Fabbrocino connected deputies of Ovitz and Burkle with Scour, who delegated the task of raising money to Kalanick.

For Kalanick it was the ultimate on-the-job training. "I was doing the deal and learning all the things that in Silicon Valley are standardized now," says Kalanick, who had neither a background in deal making nor mentors to turn to for advice. "We have blog posts now about all that stuff, about how term sheets work, for example. But at the time, nobody knew shit. It was all tribal knowledge. There was no source of information on venture deals. So you had to learn. I was living at my parents' house at the time, and I remember just being on the phone like eight hours a day."

In the spring of 1999, the group reached an agreement with

Ovitz and Burkle. The two LA power players—who were technolog-
ically ignorant but had deep pockets—would invest $4 million for a
controlling, 51 percent stake in Scour. The young company would
move into the same building in Beverly Hills as Checkout.com.
The deal was supposed to close within a month, during which time
the Scour side was not allowed to solicit a better deal, known
as a "no-shop" clause. Almost immediately, though, the entrepreneurs got cold feet, worried that they shouldn't have given up
control of their fledgling company. What's more, a record label
called GoodNoise that distributed the songs of indie bands over
the Internet had expressed interest in taking a minority stake in
Scour. At the same time, Ovitz was attempting to renegotiate
the terms of the deal, which didn't close in the intended time
frame. "I had to call Ovitz up and say look, our thirty-day no-shop
is done. We're going to have to go get funding," says Kalanick. It
wasn't an auspicious start to a relationship with one's investors.
Kalanick says Ovitz extended the no-shop clause by a few days,
also to no avail. "And one morning there was this story in *The
Wall Street Journal* saying we'd been sued by Michael Ovitz for
breaking this 'no-shop.'"

The suit came as a shock—and an education. "Very quickly,
we started realizing how this game worked," says Droege. "We
were being trained by some of the most evil people on earth—
anyone in Hollywood." The experience was profound for Kalanick, suggests Droege. "He was always intense, but we went
through this fund-raising process, and it was like one of these
life-changing moments."

Like a scene out of *The Godfather*, it dawned on the entrepreneurs that they'd been made an offer they couldn't refuse. Says Kalanick: "We took the money. We had no choice."

◉━━◉

The summer of 1999 was momentous for Scour beyond the machinations of its fund-raising. With $4 million in hand from Ovitz and Burkle, the company moved to Beverly Hills and started hiring staff. The success of its Web site—as well as its limitations—also attracted the attention of a competitor that ultimately would lead to Scour's demise. That competitor would burn brighter and longer than Scour, but fall just as hard. It was called Napster.

Scour's fundamental problem was that it didn't scale, meaning that it didn't necessarily work better the bigger it got. While its offering was compelling to young music fans, their demand for songs outstripped Scour's ability to supply them. "We got super popular," says Kalanick. "But then there were a limited number of sources of content. You'd have this limited number of boxes"—meaning, personal computers belonging to Scour's users—"that had a Britney Spears song," he explains. (The singer had released her first smash-hit album, . . . *Baby One More Time,* in 1999.) "Too many people were going after the same content and boxes would crash. Then, when you'd search for the link, you'd get your link and you'd click and it wouldn't work because the box on the other side was crashed." Scour's engineers then scurried to remove bad links and also to crawl the Internet for fresh sources of music. New content led to spikes in traffic. "But then we'd run out of content," says Kalanick, and the cycle would begin again.

As is often the case with disruptive technologies, Scour's shortcomings led a rival entrepreneur to hit on a small innovation that made a big difference. Scour allowed users to see what music other users had in their library. To listen to a song they wanted to hear, however, they had to request it, triggering a file transfer from one user to another via the network. Shawn Fanning, like many of Scour's users, was obsessed with music and technology. He figured out what Scour was missing, and in May 1999, about eighteen months after the UCLA computer pals had founded Scour, Fanning and Sean Parker built Napster to be a better file-sharing mousetrap. "He was like, 'Why not when I pull a file down from Scour don't I just automatically share it?'" recalls Kalanick, referring to a technique whereby listening to a song would automatically make it available to every other user. What's more, because Napster only showed users what was currently available, it didn't have Scour's problem of overpromising and underdelivering. "And that was Napster. It basically was Scour, and then he tweaked it, and that little tweak changed everything." Kalanick and Fanning would become friends, and Fanning would be one of Uber's early investors. Kalanick, mindful of what Napster did to Scour, would never forget the importance of rapidly innovating on a competitor's good ideas. More than a decade later when he saw Lyft out-innovate Uber, he reacted quickly.

Napster became a viral sensation and a part of the cultural conversation. It quickly outshined Scour: by 2001 it had been downloaded 80 million times. Scour, in comparison, had 7 million downloads at its peak. Scour was now in a position to play catch-up, and it rolled out a service called Scour Exchange, which worked a lot like Napster. (The success of both companies rested on allowing users to listen to music—and in the case of Scour, watch movies—they didn't own. Soon enough this would haunt them both.) For its part, Scour tried mightily to keep up. It created a marketing campaign aimed squarely at the young people who were its target market. Its methods for promoting Scour Exchange, SX for short, were in character for a company run by a bunch of young men. Scour hired a marketing firm that hit campuses nationwide to hand out bottles of personal-care lubricant with a sticker that screamed Scour Exchange's provocative slogan: "For smooth downloads use SX."

Scour succeeded in gaining attention. In November 1999, the streaming-file software company RealNetworks tried to buy it, a move favored by its controlling shareholders. That same month several recording studios banded together to sue the now bigger Napster, charging that its peer-to-peer music downloading service enabled copyright infringement. Especially if Real could figure out a legal way to market the Scour Exchange, selling out represented a good financial result. The founders, however, would have ended up as Real employees, holding stock rather than cash in return for selling. In the middle of the negotiations the tech news site *CNET*, citing "a source familiar with the plan," reported that Real planned to pay $100 million for Scour. "Someone decided to leak to the press that we were being purchased, I think to torpedo the offer," says Haykinson. "They were offering whatever they were offering, and someone leaked that they were offering something well above anything they were willing to pay us. So it certainly looked like a well-placed call to a reporter basically killed that deal." The neophytes, who'd been shocked mere months earlier by reading in the newspaper that they were being sued by Ovitz, showed they had mastered the art of negotiating through the news media.

Not selling turned out to have been a missed opportunity, given what was happening to Napster. The entertainment industry viewed Napster as an existential threat. Young people who believed music was free wouldn't buy music anymore. And once Internet broadband improved, as the film studios understood it would, their DVD market would be in the same peril. In July 2000, three entertainment trade associations filed a copyright infringement suit against Scour, leveling similar charges to the ones Napster was battling: Scour Exchange facilitated illegal downloads of movies and music. The requested damages—a per-infringement amount that added up to $250 billion—were intended to kill Scour.

Most irksome to Scour's young executives was that many of the movie studios were paying Scour to promote their films at the same time their lawyers were suing them. "On one call they were like, 'Hey, how many downloads did we get yesterday? How much exposure did we get on that?'" says Droege. "And then on another call it'd be, 'Hey, we're going to sue you guys out of business.' So that was pretty weird."

While Napster's case dragged on for years—it wouldn't file for bankruptcy until 2002—Scour met its demise in a matter of months. Some of its founders, particularly Kalanick, wanted to fight. But he had little money and therefore little to lose. That wasn't the case for Burkle and, particularly, Ovitz, whose livelihood was tied to the very industry that was battling Scour. (A partner at one of Napster's venture-capital investors in San Francisco, an ex-lawyer named Hank Barry, became CEO of Napster and fought for it to stay in business.) Various firms, including Liquid Audio and Listen.com, bid at auction for Scour's assets, with Scour's founders present in the courtroom for the legal proceedings. Says Kalanick: "You're watching your work, your stuff being auctioned off in a bankruptcy court. And there's no ceremony. It's just brute-force efficiency. That's how bankruptcy court rolls." Ultimately, a Portland, Oregon, company named Center-Span Communications won the auction, purchasing Scour's assets for $9 million, intending to operate Scour Exchange as a legitimate file-sharing service. Several Scour founders consulted for CenterSpan for some months in the hopes of salvaging the business, but little came of the assets CenterSpan bought.

For all the founders, including Kalanick, it was yet another learning experience, if not a pleasant one. One lesson was the need to develop an explanation for public consumption. "My line was that we were declaring Chapter 11 as a strategic move as a result of the lawsuit," he reflects. "When you try to seem positive about something that actually is quite depressing, it starts to get hard to wake up in the morning. You literally start sleeping, at least in my case, twelve hours a day, fourteen hours a day. It's a super un-fun experience. That was the first time I realized life's too short to put a happy face on when it's not a happy situation."

It may not have been a happy ending, but already Kalanick was becoming battle tested. Technology companies needed scale, both to fend off the competition and to make users keep coming back for more. As well, choosing whom to take money from and how to maintain control of one's company were worthy goals for any entrepreneur. Achieving scale, raising cash, and keeping his hands on the proverbial steering wheel would become near obsessions for Kalanick a decade later, at Uber.

Yet by the end of 2000 Scour was all but gone, and twenty-four-year-old Travis Kalanick, like his closest friends from UCLA, had no college degree and no job. He would need a new plan—and fast.

CHAPTER 3
Lean Times

Scour's demise essentially marked the first time Kalanick was out of work since he was a child. Though his first truly adult business experience had just ended, he already was a hardened member of the cult of the entrepreneur. Like Steve Jobs, whose family wrote "entrepreneur" in the box for occupation on his death certificate, Kalanick defined himself as someone whose destiny and joy were starting businesses. After all, in his estimation, two of the most important qualities to be an entrepreneur were creativity and stubbornness.

Stubbornness appears to have been hardwired. Like many boys his age, he participated with his father in a program run by the YMCA called Indian Guides. All Guides and their dads had "Indian" names. Kalanick's was "Laughing Wolf"—because, he says, "I was always laughing"—and his father was "Crazy Wolf." (A disclosure feels necessary: in a different part of the country and a decade earlier, my father and I were "Big Bear" and "Little Bear," respectively, in the same YMCA program.) The Guides were a product of their time, an opportunity for breadwinner dads to spend time with their sons, especially outdoors. (An equally politically incorrectly named program for dads and their daughters was called Indian Princesses. The Y has since struck the word "Indian" from both.) Yet what Kalanick remembers most from his Guides experience isn't hanging with his dad, but rather his prowess selling tickets to a pancake breakfast fund-raiser. "I was always the top seller," he recounts, with no small amount of satisfaction, some thirty years later. "So I'd go in front of the Hughes supermarket at like two P.M., and I'd be selling pancake breakfast tickets dressed like a fricking Indian. And I would go to eleven P.M. I would just go until my parents would tear me away from the place."

His burning need to outsell the other little boys notwith-standing, Kalanick's childhood was exceedingly routine. He played baseball and football, loved math, ran track, and relied on his older sisters to help him be cool, especially when it came to picking the right clothes. He credits his father, Don, a civil engi-neer for the city of Los Angeles who worked on many projects at Los Angeles International Airport, with instilling in him an en-gineer's mind-set. A tinkerer, Don Kalanick liked to take things apart and put them back together again. "He doesn't call a plumber, he just fixes it," says Kalanick. "He doesn't call some-body to fix the air-conditioning, he opens it up and figures it out. That's just how he rolls." He calls his mother, Bonnie, who sold newspaper ads, the more emotive and people-oriented of his par-ents. "She would take us home from school every day and tell us how much she loved us. And then she would tell us the one thing that mattered to her is that we never do drugs. And to this day I've never done drugs."

The Kalanicks were neither rich nor poor, though there were times when money was tight. Neither rich nor poor is also an apt description for Northridge, the San Fernando Valley town where they lived. It is a close-in LA suburb of modest bungalows that was, in Kalanick's words, "just right down the middle of the middle." Most of the clan stayed that way. Kalanick's older sisters, both from his father's previous marriage, later sold skin-care products and worked at a copy shop. His brother Cory, younger by eleven months, is a firefighter in Fresno, in California's Central Valley. (Cory is something of a celebrity, if not in his older brother's league: a 2013 YouTube video of him saving a kitten from a burning home went viral, making him a local hero.) Among Kalanick's close relations are more firefighters, a handful of teachers, a social worker, and a physical therapist. Says Kalanick: "This is not like Yale. That's not my family."

Family vacations meant camping. Says Kalanick: "Through high school my dad, me, and my brother would go into the Sierras for a week every summer, and we would eat what we caught. You learn all the nuances of cooking fish. Because it's fish for breakfast, lunch, and dinner. So you're like, put the salt on thirty-five seconds after you start to cook it, then the butter right at the end."

Despite their middle-class life, one thing Kalanick's father splurged on was computers. "We always had the latest and greatest, whether it was a Commodore 64 or an Apple II," he says. His dad used the computers to teach him math ahead of his grade level, and Kalanick recalls being enough of a math nerd that he got picked on for it. "I was geeky enough to get bullied. Not like physically beat up really, but just made fun of, ostracized." Reflecting on his public battles with taxi companies and regulators he has accused of being corrupt, he says, "That could be where the justice thing comes from."

Kalanick was a geek in a jock's body. He played third base in baseball and defensive back in football in grade school. In high school, he ran track. His favorite event was the 400-meter relay. "I was never the fastest at the four hundred, but they always put me on the anchor leg. Because if there was somebody in front of me I would catch them."

When Kalanick wasn't playing sports, he was working. He scooped ice cream at Baskin-Robbins and made copies at Kinko's. He had a job conducting telephone surveys. "I'm the one calling, trying to get somebody to stay on the phone for thirty minutes where you ask them questions. It was like a boiler room." He didn't necessarily work out of an inordinate craving for money. Pressed for the source of his drive, Kalanick comes up with two explanations. His father, he says, has an "insane" work ethic, which seems to have rubbed off. "My dad grew up poor," he says. Other than emulating his father, Kalanick chalks up his entrepreneurial hustle, even as a kid, to the same competitive streak that made him the anchor runner in track. "There's this entrepreneurial thing, like, 'I work harder than you,'" he says. "A lot of entrepreneurs start out that way. It comes from an insecurity. Like maybe you aren't making ends meet and you need to act tough to make it through."

Some of Kalanick's youthful jobs prepared him for the

executive he'd become. He sold knives, for example, through a company that essentially was a multilevel marketing scheme. "You start with your mom and your friends and sell their moms knives, and then you get referrals as part of the sale, and then you just start working it." For the future engineer, the experience was revelatory. "Engineers judge sales. They think it's cheesy and not grounded. But it's also storytelling. That's the thing you learn in sales. You learn how to tell a story."

Kalanick kept working after starting at UCLA, where he was originally on a five-year plan that would have earned him degrees in two majors. A combined computer science and electrical engineering was one. Business economics was the other. In the period just before joining Scour, he had three internships that exposed him to the ways of big business: a summertime job with a consulting firm in San Francisco called Silicon Valley Internet Partners; the Intel assignment in Oregon; and the Boston Consulting Group stint, where his client was Southern California Edison. But his longest-standing and most unusual part-time job was the SAT prep class he helped start near his parents' home, New Way Academy. Barely a year older than his students, Kalanick would put on a tie and spend his Saturdays lecturing mostly Korean high school students on how to achieve high test scores. "Teaching sixteen-year-olds and seventeen-year-olds, the only way to make it work is to make it a performance," he says. "You're doing eight hours of performance, and you have to be on your toes. You have to be funny, you have to be quick, you have to be clever. You have to be able to shoot people down who are being disruptive. The whole thing."

With all these youthful experiences, even before the time the first start-up Kalanick had been involved with failed, he had learned the importance of storytelling, the art of performance, and the humiliation of begging for money. He was on his way to being an entrepreneur.

◉─────────────────────────────────────◉

The judge had barely banged the gavel finalizing the disposal of Scour when Kalanick and Todd began hatching their next company. Like singers whose next songs sound a lot like their last ones, the pair didn't stray far from the themes they'd been pursuing since UCLA. They essentially recreated Scour, but with a critical twist. Their new company, Red Swoosh, would be legally unassailable—in this instance, at least, Kalanick found it expedient to keep the lawyers at bay—and focused on business customers, not consumers. In fact, Kalanick and Todd planned to offer their technology to the very entertainment companies that had sued Scour. (There would later be grumbling that Red Swoosh used Scour's software code, which Kalanick and others say wasn't the case.)

Whereas Scour had allowed individuals to use their computers and the Internet to share songs and videos, Red Swoosh would enable companies to use the Internet to share similarly large files with their customers. Facilitating the movement of large files was already a big business, led by companies like Akamai, Exodus Communications, and Digital Island. These companies deployed massive and expensive computer networks to serve their clients, many of whom were media companies that wanted to be able to deliver programs, movie trailers, and the like quickly over the Web.

With Kalanick as CEO, this time a true founder, and Todd as chief technology officer, the new company began with an overt nod to its predecessor: Scour's logo had been two red swooshes formed into an *S*. Red Swoosh's software would do what Akamai and the others did but more cheaply and with several bells and whistles the incumbent players didn't offer. According to a document prepared for prospective investors just three months after the company started, Red Swoosh would call itself an "edge delivery network." (The lingo favored by the incumbent players was "content delivery network," or CDN.) The "edge" in Red Swoosh's scheme, and the key to its offering, was the "peer-to-peer" trick that powered Scour: Red Swoosh would harness the power of individual PCs connected to the public Internet. (These inexpensive PCs, belonging to client companies and their customers, weren't part of a company's network. They were on the "edge" of the network.) The company's March 2001 investor prospectus, a sort of road map for a journey barely begun, explained that the "Red Swoosh solution is not dependent on massive investments in thousands of servers or dozens of data centers deployed close to the edge throughout the world. Instead, Red Swoosh leverages the massive unused capacity of the desktop to share and deliver content inexpensively, effectively, and legally."

What is remarkable about Red Swoosh's plan isn't just its tweak on the commercially attractive aspects of Scour, but how it foreshadowed the so-called asset-light strategy that would be Uber's secret sauce. Just as Red Swoosh software would push and pull files from personal computers owned by others, Uber one day would connect riders with drivers whose cars represented "massive unused capacity" on the streets of cities. Where Red Swoosh dreamed that the "unused capacity of the desktop PC represents 3,000 times the available capacity at all the CDNs worldwide," Uber would eventually assemble a fleet it didn't own that would dwarf the number of cars operated by any competing taxi service. In short, Scour and Red Swoosh represented, at least for Travis Kalanick, a direct through-line to Uber.

Most audacious of all was how the young entrepreneurs managed to salvage relationships with the very companies they'd clashed with only months earlier. The irony was lost on no one. "It's like a drug dealer becoming a pharmacist," reflects Francesco Fabbrocino, the UCLA friend of Michael Todd's who became an early employee of Red Swoosh. Engaging the entertainment titans also offered a shot at redemption. "It was really cool because we were going to all of these content owners' offices," says Kalanick. "We'd get super-high-level meetings with like thirty people attending at Disney." Curiosity trumped animosity as far as the entertainment companies were concerned. It was the same year Apple debuted its digital "jukebox" software iTunes, which in 2003 would become a legal alternative to Napster. The music and film companies needed all the technological intelligence they could get. Remembers Kalanick: "They were like, 'Didn't we fucking sue you guys out of business? And now you're trying to sell us this shit? Oh well, show us what you've got. We just want to see it.'"

As a first-time CEO, albeit for a company whose employees could fit into a midsize sedan, it was Kalanick's job to pitch potential clients. Despite his theatrical experiences teaching college-prep courses, he sometimes got nervous in front of a crowd. "We presented at Disney, and he was shaking while he talked," remembers Fabbrocino, Red Swoosh's head of engineering. "I said, 'Dude, calm down. People will think you're lying.'" Kalanick did calm down, Fabbrocino remembers. "Travis was surprisingly good at feedback."

Kalanick set a frenetic, workaholic tone at Red Swoosh, one that would be familiar a few years later to his employees at Uber. "That guy was on his phone 24/7," recalls Fabbrocino. "He would pace, and we would yell at him to stop." Kalanick was frugal as well, sometimes in eccentric ways. He rode an old motorcycle to work, in all kinds of weather. Says Fabbrocino: "We all thought he was crazy. Sometimes he would show up for work drenched from the rain. I respected that." There was a less attractive side to Kalanick's thriftiness. "Every now and then we would go to lunch, and he'd forget his wallet," says Fabbrocino.

Such small recollections would add up over the years to a sense of shiftiness about Kalanick, a can't-quite-put-your-finger-on-it untrustworthiness that would irk some who dealt with him. "He'd write a large dollar figure on the whiteboard, circling it and outlining it for effect, just in case somebody came by and saw it," remembers Ilya Haykinson, the early Scour engineer who joined Kalanick and Todd at Red Swoosh. "You knew that was the only reason it was written there. That's kind of a weird, sleazy move. It's not bad. But it has no meaning. It's just for show."

In fact, big dollar signs were in short supply for most of Red Swoosh's existence. The Internet bubble peaked in the spring of 2000, and the tiny company, begun in early 2001, was affected in two ways. First, the plummeting valuations of the established competitors Red Swoosh was targeting bode ill for its fundraising ambitions. If Akamai, for example, was worth billions of dollars less than a year earlier, the perceived opportunity of attacking it was much smaller. Worse, traditional sources of funding for start-up technology companies, especially those run by teams of youthful entrepreneurs whose last start-up had flamed out, had dried up. Kalanick met with a venture capitalist in Silicon Valley—a perennial challenge was the dearth of tech investors in Southern California—who told him he'd felt there was no more innovation left to be invented in software. "It was the most irrationally cynical thing you could ever imagine. It was just a sign of the times." Kalanick was experiencing the herd mentality that drives venture-capital funding cycles. Silicon Valley investors often would rather invest in five online pet stores than one unique venture. For better or worse, the small Red Swoosh team was pursuing the only business it knew with the only potential clients that would grant them meetings.

The former Scour team did, however, have one unconventional source of income. The company that bought Scour's assets needed help understanding and managing what they'd acquired. Todd signed a consulting contract with CenterSpan and farmed out some of the work to Red Swoosh employees. "We did a services contract to keep the data center up and running, things like that," says Kalanick. "That's how we paid the bills at the beginning."

How exactly Red Swoosh paid its employees would become a source of tension. Haykinson says that because he was working on CenterSpan projects on Red Swoosh's time, he'd funnel his

CenterSpan payments directly to Red Swoosh and in return get stock in the start-up. "It was weird," he says. "But it worked."

The contracting arrangement led to confusion, however, as to the status of Red Swoosh's employees. Even with the Center-Span money, cash was tight, and the company stopped making payroll deductions. This was a violation of Internal Revenue Service requirements. It was also a red flag for potential investors. Michael Todd says everyone at the company knew about the withholding decision—and that he disagreed with it. "I thought it was a bad idea to not pay payroll taxes. We all talked about this." What's more, Todd was concerned that he'd personally be on the hook for the withholding liability.

Kalanick saw Todd as the culprit. "He was handling all the accounting. The way I describe it is incompetence. We owed the U.S. government like a hundred grand. That's like a white-collar-crime situation." Kalanick believed Todd was trying to sell Red Swoosh without telling him. "We obviously weren't able to get funding, and we didn't have any real paying customers yet," he says. "And we're eight months in." Todd, suggests Kalanick, simply didn't have the stomach for start-up life. "So I basically kicked him out of the company." For his part, Todd says he couldn't have sold Red Swoosh without Kalanick's approval given that they started as fifty-fifty partners. He also disputes having been kicked out, saying he left of his own volition.

What had been a friendly combination of technical smarts and business hustle devolved into finger pointing and bad blood. Kalanick would identify himself in e-mails as the "Founder, CEO" of Red Swoosh. "It bugged Mike that he said 'founder' and not 'cofounder,'" says Rob Reagan, who'd later invest in Red Swoosh.

In time, several of Scour's alumni joined Todd at Google, where he worked next, and then at an advertising-technology company he joined called OpenX. Todd hung on to his stake in Red Swoosh, however, and would eventually be glad he did.

Off to an inauspicious start, Red Swoosh knew tragedy before it was a year old. On September 11, 2001, Kalanick had planned to meet with Danny Lewin, a cofounder and chief technology officer of Akamai, about a potential partnership that might have led to an acquisition. An Israeli-American who served in an elite Israel Defense Forces antiterrorism unit, Lewin was on board doomed American Airlines Flight 11 from Boston to Los Angeles, which crashed into the north tower of the World Trade Center. Lewin is believed to be the first person to die on 9/11, having risen from his seat to confront one of the hijackers, only to have his throat slit from behind by another terrorist. Says Fabbrocino: "It was dark times."

By late 2001, even as Red Swoosh continued to develop its product, its financial situation grew more precarious. "We ran out of money," says Kalanick, at a time Red Swoosh was in arrears to the IRS and its employees. "Then the services contract with that company that bought Scour stopped." Traditional VC firms weren't an option. And Kalanick also got nowhere talking to his bigger competitors, who were facing cash constraints of their own. "I mean, this all just got super fucked up."

◉──◉

It quickly became apparent just how unreal the times had been just a couple years earlier, when Kalanick and his UCLA buddies had so easily raised $4 million from Michael Ovitz and Ron Burkle. Then the money flowed, even for a company without much of a business run by a bunch of guys with no experience. That was before the dot-com bust, before 9/11, and before the recession that followed. Now, with a slightly more seasoned crew and an idea in a sector that was a proven moneymaker, Red Swoosh had a tough time simply getting meetings. Says Kalanick: "I was just trying to hustle and do whatever I could."

A reprieve came from an obscure source. In late 2001, Kalanick found a small Southern California venture-capital firm run by a semiconductor entrepreneur named James Chao and his son, Jared. The elder Chao had made a fortune starting a company that made components for military-grade communications systems and selling it for hundreds of millions of dollars. The younger Chao was a recent law school graduate and the same age as Red Swoosh's founders. The father-and-son team started an investment firm, Chaos Venture Partners, named not for a love of disorder but because there were two "Chaos" involved.

Kalanick, trained in the art of hardball negotiation at the knee of Michael Ovitz, taught himself how to negotiate from a position of weakness. His company, after all, had no cash, no customers, and some onerous obligations. He learned, he says, how to "breadcrumb" a deal, also known as "saving the worst for the last." Chaos planned to lend Red Swoosh $300,000, with its debt potentially turning into a 10 percent ownership position. The venture firm checked in with Disney, which validated its interest in Red Swoosh's technology, and was prepared to do a deal.

At this point Kalanick chose to explain to his prospective investor that the company had a few problems, or "excepts," in

Kalanick's argot. It was akin to a real estate agent waiting until the last moment to spring a disclosure of a termite infestation on a checkbook-wielding home buyer. "You get them hooked as much as you can, and then you go, 'Hey dude, I've just got to let you know, there are a few 'excepts,'" Kalanick recounts. "Except, we owe the U.S. government a hundred grand. Except, we owe my own employees a hundred grand. And this was like the last thing right before we're supposed to get this thing done."

Chaos wasn't pleased to know two thirds of its loan would leave the company's coffers right away. So it tripled the potential stake in Red Swoosh that it would get for its money. Kalanick had no breadcrumbs left. "They said, 'Well, instead of ten percent of the company, we think we should get thirty percent of the company for our three hundred grand.' And I'm like, 'Sounds good.' And so on the Friday after Thanksgiving in 2001, I closed three hundred grand, two hundred grand of which went out the door immediately."

This was the first of what became a string of dodging-and-weaving negotiations Kalanick would engage in over the course of Red Swoosh's history, some of which worked out better than others. Soon after, he began talking to Cable & Wireless, a British telecommunications operator that could offer Red Swoosh's technology to its customers. "They were interested in this disruptive technology where you could basically get free bandwidth," he explains. "We were in advanced discussions, but they were just taking their sweet time. And then I basically had to call a meeting with them. I call it the take-your-toys-and-go-home close, which is, 'Hey guys, I know you're super interested in our technology, but I'm running out of money. And unless we can figure out a way for you to fund this, you're not going to be able to play with this toy.'" Cable & Wireless bit, signing a $150,000 deal with Red Swoosh. "Then I could pay people again," says Kalanick.

And so it continued. In early 2002, Kalanick says he succeeded in attracting the interest of August Capital, which planned to invest $10 million in Red Swoosh. August was the type of firm Kalanick had long coveted. An established, pedigreed firm on Sand Hill Road in Menlo Park, California, August was best known for having made an early and extremely lucrative investment in Microsoft. Landing an investment from August would confer legitimacy on the upstart company. But August had two conditions in return for its investment. First, it wanted Red Swoosh to find another, similar firm to coinvest alongside it. Second, it suggested that Kalanick cede the CEO position to a more seasoned executive, a common VC demand known as requiring "adult supervision."

August agreed to invest $500,000 right away as Kalanick continued to seek other investors. The VC firm then tapped from its network a former Exodus Communications executive named Robert Bowman to be CEO. He took over immediately, with Kalanick becoming executive chairman, a way of being shoved aside without being fired. Bowman was in many ways a more seasoned version of Kalanick, who remembers him as "a super hard-core guy and a workaholic. He smoked like two packs a day and drank like five pots of coffee. He was super intense."

Kalanick also found a venture outfit to co-invest with August. It was Steamboat Ventures, a corporate investing arm of Disney. Steamboat wasn't acceptable to August Capital, though, which feared the Disney investment might scare off potential customers that were Disney competitors. With no coinvestor in sight, August said it wouldn't make a large investment in Red Swoosh after all. Kalanick did manage to get a $100,000 loan from August, as part of what he called a "parting gift." He used half of August's overall investment to buy out Chaos, and he moved Red Swoosh to Palo Alto to be closer to Bowman. Red Swoosh now had a little money to play with, an experienced executive at the helm, and a big-name VC as a backer, albeit in a minor way.

All this still wasn't enough. With the economy not improving much, Red Swoosh's employees started leaving. The company floundered, and the newly arrived Bowman left after less than a year, getting out of the technology business altogether for a time. With money running low again and having moved back to LA, Red Swoosh was down to two people, Kalanick and an engineer named Evan Tsang, who had been an early employee at Scour as well. "From the fall of 2002 until 2005 it was just me and him," Kalanick recounts. "I had two customers. I had this company, iFilm, which was paying us five grand a month, and I had IGN"— a video game Web site—"paying us five grand a month. We were always just one big deal away from making it. There was always somebody earnestly interested in doing something big." Kalanick says at one point he signed a distributor of pornography to what was a major deal for the struggling company, $18,000 a month. "But," he says, "they never paid."

Kalanick had one fleeting shot at selling Red Swoosh during these lean times, in what would have been an honorable if modest outcome. In the middle of 2003, Microsoft approached him about buying Red Swoosh so that the software giant could integrate peer-to-peer capability into its operating system. According to Kalanick, Microsoft first offered an embarrassingly low price, a bit over $1 million. He rejected that offer but quickly reached agreement on a better price, $5 million. Then, he says, "it just got killed at the last minute," a not uncommon occurrence for corporate M&A activity. "It was super heartbreaking."

The sensible thing for Kalanick to have done at this point would have been to have packed it in and looked for a job. Comparing Red Swoosh to an abusive spouse, however, he says he couldn't let go. "I just believed." His persistence left an impression. "Travis was a young, manic guy who had a vision," says David Hornik, a venture capitalist at August Capital. "The more excited he got about it the faster he talked about it. He was convinced that this was the way content should be distributed and make the Web better. Every time I talked to Travis he continued to be energetic around trying to make the idea work. He's a never-say-die entrepreneur. He was never willing to admit defeat. His attitude was: 'I'm going to make this work.'"

In early 2005, Kalanick got an important nibble: AOL, the then powerful Internet service, was close to signing a significant deal. That January, despite running a two-person company that was perennially one step away from insolvency, he was invited to attend the World Economic Forum in Davos, Switzerland, as a "tech pioneer," a kind of nonpaying attendee with glorified intern status at the prestigious schmoozefest. There he met with Paul Sagan, the CEO of Akamai. "He sought me out," says Sagan. "He always assumed Akamai would buy his business."

Things were finally looking up for Red Swoosh. Kalanick says his agreement with AOL was "a breakthrough deal where they were going to pay over a million dollars a year for our services and I'd go from two people to something bigger." But while Kalanick was in Davos, Michael Todd helped recruit Red Swoosh's only employee, Evan Tsang, to Google. AOL promptly backed out of the deal. "They said I lost my last engineer and it was just me."

Kalanick had an uncanny ability to find investors, however. For several years he had been corresponding by e-mail with billionaire Internet entrepreneur Mark Cuban. How the two met illustrates Kalanick's networking acumen. There was a restaurant in LA's Chinatown neighborhood called Pho 87 that hosted weekend chats for people interested in music technology. The organizer of the chats, a record technology executive named Jim Griffin, built an online discussion forum called the Pho List. Kalanick and Cuban were members, and they frequently traded barbed comments on the site, each being pugnacious and opinionated. In need of money and support, Kalanick turned to Cuban, telling him about the AOL deal. Cuban agreed to invest in Red Swoosh—the board of directors became Kalanick and Cuban—and to help Kalanick with AOL's business, which he eventually won. Again, Kalanick moved Red Swoosh to the Bay Area, this time to the unglamorous suburb of San Mateo, midway between Palo Alto and San Francisco. With Cuban's money he was able to staff up a bit to go after more deals.

The company had some prospects now, but it was also small enough to engage in bouts of whimsy. In 2006, with Red Swoosh's lease expiring in San Mateo, Kalanick suggested that the band of about six engineers act on what had been the kind of goofy scheme a bunch of colleagues cooked up over a few beers. They should, he said, move the whole company to some exotic beach— one with reliable Internet service—and work there for some period of time. The group put a few names in a hat. The winner was Thailand, and within a few days all of Red Swoosh was off to Bangkok, still not knowing where they'd end up. They found their way to Railay Beach, near Krabi. "And we coded there for two months." They only returned, Kalanick says, because some of the guys had girlfriends back home. "So it got complicated."

By 2007, Kalanick was on the verge of landing a deal with EchoStar, the satellite television company, which wanted to offer a streaming product. Cuban had decided he wanted out of Red Swoosh, however, and completing a deal without the support of his investor was going to be tough. So Kalanick found a venture firm, Crosslink Capital, that agreed to buy out Cuban's stake, which also enabled him to do the deal with EchoStar. It was around this time that Akamai, its own fortunes having recovered from the depths of the dot-com bust, finally became interested in buying Red Swoosh. Despite its meager revenues, the tiny start-up offered Akamai the opportunity to build in certain peer-to-peer technical capabilities its own engineers had resisted. There still wasn't much to Red Swoosh, but it held promise, both for having built up some technology whose time was finally arriving and because of its mind-set that was anything but corporate. "Swoosh was a way to hire a bunch of pirates to get it done," says Sagan, then Akamai's CEO. "In many ways what we bought was a cultural model."

Akamai agreed to pay Red Swoosh $18.7 million, and Kalanick was on the threshold of his first success as an entrepreneur.

Just as the sale represented redemption for Kalanick, it would prove to be a bittersweet victory for Red Swoosh's other cofounder, Michael Todd. Ilya Haykinson, who remained in touch with both Red Swoosh cofounders, remembers there being concern in the Red Swoosh alumni community that Todd would hobble the deal out of spite. Standing to make considerable money himself, Todd did nothing of the sort. "He told me, 'I'm not going to say no to a million dollars.'"

In April 2007, Akamai agreed to buy Red Swoosh, which meant hiring its handful of employees, including Kalanick. His personal deal with Akamai was to stay for three years. "I did one," he says.

CHAPTER 4
Jamming

O nce again, Travis Kalanick was at a transition point in his career, this time under more favorable circumstances than when Scour cratered six years earlier. Now thirty-one years old, for the first time in his life he had real money in his pocket: his take from selling to Akamai was about $3 million. Still, he wasn't yet free to do something new. For the time being, at least, he had a real job. And also for the first time other than his college internships, he would be an employee of an established company.

In the technology industry, big companies are forever buying little ones. Typically, the buyer isn't interested in revenue or sales leads, and sometimes it isn't even concerned with existing products. Often, buyers want the people. Akamai's Paul Sagan acknowledged as much as his motivation for buying Red Swoosh. He was after the outlaw Kalanick and his small band of engineers who were conversant in a new type of technology and unafraid to buck Akamai's larger engineering corps to build it. "I used the rebellious nature of Travis and Swoosh to get something done that I had been banging my head against the wall to do for years," says Sagan, referring to his desire to build peer-to-peer software into Akamai's bundle of offerings. "We had a not-invented-here problem. Travis was his usual, brash self, which was irksome to some but also helpful"—particularly to Sagan.

Kalanick had his own agenda. At least initially, he saw the buyout as an opportunity to continue building Red Swoosh, which had preoccupied him for most of his twenties. He maintained the office Red Swoosh had opened in San Francisco and kept working on its software. He struggled, he says, to deflect intrusions from folks at Akamai's headquarters near Boston. "When you're doing a start-up inside of a big company you can put a moat around it, like make it hard to have lots of meetings," he says. "We were the sexy thing for the company, and everybody wanted a piece. So we really tried to keep distractions low and fend off people. Eventually they breached the moat. And when that happened it was time to leave."

Entrepreneurs exiting the company that bought them is par for the course in the technology industry, so Kalanick wasn't burning bridges by bolting. (He did, however, leave a small amount of money on the table in the form of unrealized stock options.) Departing Akamai in late 2008, he was suddenly unattached to any one company. Moreover, he lived at a time of global economic turmoil and in a city on the cusp of a significant transition. Though Kalanick's personal fortune had brightened, the rest of the world, including a good portion of the start-up community, was in peril. Wall Street was in the depths of a financial crisis triggered by the U.S. housing market's collapse, America had entered what would become known as the Great Recession, and venture-capital funding was, yet again, scarce.

Paradoxically, this season of international discontent coincided with a springlike blossoming among the community of technology companies in San Francisco proper. The region's most important urban center long had been a mere footnote in the information-technology narrative. "Silicon Valley," though literally a concept rather than a geographic area, loosely referred to a stretch of suburban towns along the 101 freeway from Palo Alto to San Jose, more than fifty miles south of San Francisco. Nearly every important tech company of the twentieth century had started there, frequently with a connection to nearby Stanford University and often to the defense-industry communications equipment companies that emerged after World War II. While San Francisco was the region's financial and cultural hub—techies went there to party and shop—its suburbs gave rise to all the biggest and most influential companies. These included Hewlett-Packard (in Palo Alto), Intel (Santa Clara), Apple (Cupertino), and Cisco Systems (San Jose). The first crop of major Internet companies hunted for engineering talent in its natural habitat, in "the Valley," and they started there too. Yahoo (Sunnyvale), Google (Mountain View), and Facebook (Menlo Park) all followed this playbook.

San Francisco wasn't a complete tech wasteland. A large handful of smaller Internet companies, most with some connection to media or advertising technology, had formed in San Francisco during the dot-com bubble of the late 1990s. Most vanished just as quickly. Then, in the depth of one of the tech industry's periodic down cycles, something changed. One new software company, Salesforce.com, grew rapidly in San Francisco, primarily because of its founder's preference for urban living. Then, as Google and other tech giants began offering free, Wi-Fi-enabled shuttle buses to the suburbs in order to appeal to younger city dwellers, San Francisco enjoyed a resurgence. Once that happened, more companies sprang up there. It helped that the new cluster of start-ups focused on software applications, typically for Web sites and later smartphones, needed few resources to get going, unlike the capital-intensive enterprises of the earlier era. This meant they could grow in cramped city offices and despite a funding drought. Twitter was the first runaway San Francisco success story of this era. Others followed, as young engineers came to understand they didn't have to schlep to Mountain View or Menlo Park to have interesting and high-paying jobs.

It was into this milieu that Kalanick launched himself on a new, temporary career as an "angel" investor and adviser to entrepreneurs. So-called angels were a new phenomenon. Their stakes in companies, usually several tens of thousands of dollars each, were less than the smallest investment a venture capitalist would make. "Real" VCs invested from institutional funds raised from university endowments and retirement funds. In contrast, the angels were amateurs, dilettantes even. They invested their own money while playing guardian angel to a group of fledgling entrepreneurs. Their investment rationale was based more on instinct or friendship than on sophisticated financial or technical analysis.

Kalanick, with his gift for gab and hard-earned business chops— *The Guardian* once observed that he talks "like a surfer but thinks like a salesman"—took to the role quickly. A relative newcomer to San Francisco, he struck up friendships with other young entrepreneurs in town, many of whom were transplants too. He bought a house in the Castro, an old San Francisco neighborhood that was neither trendy nor posh, and he gave it a name, the JamPad. The moniker spoke volumes about Kalanick's cool guy-cum-nerd sensibilities. He fashioned his house as a hub for entrepreneurs, a bigger and more comfortable version of the Undergraduate Computer Science Association at UCLA, a place where friends could hang out and "jam" on ideas.

After so many years as the plucky entrepreneur, one step away from either success or moving back in with his parents, Kalanick was ready to reflect for a bit—and to share the lessons he had learned. He became a popular scribe for this community as well. With time on his hands, he would take to Twitter to talk about matters as mundane as going for a run or which flight he was boarding. A prolific writer—his blog was called *Swooshing*—he offered plentiful free advice to the entrepreneurial community, from how to raise money to how to market products. For one San Francisco conference popular with upstart entrepreneurs, he even offered a free place to sleep. "Making your company a success is all about being scrappy," he wrote in 2009. "Paying for hotels can crush your cash flow, so couch-surfing is the only way to go. The JamPad is the ultimate way to couch-hop in luxury & style and in a creative, entrepreneurial atmosphere." The future scourge of taxi companies and villain of the international media wanted to be known as a lovable host. "The JamPad is my San Francisco home," he wrote on his blog. "It is a place where entrepreneurs regularly come to hang out, to rap on ideas, to jam with other entrepreneurs, to play Wii Tennis and Gears of War, and to have fantastic healthy gourmet meals made by the JamPad's in-house chef. Normal open hours for the JamPad are from 10AM to 2AM. We also do BBQs, grill seshes, art & wine events, networked Armagetron competitions, coding seshes, you name it."

Kalanick's use of the word "jam" reflected the new dominant vibe in San Francisco. To an earlier generation, jamming meant coming together to play music. Kalanick's music was technology, and more specifically the software that fueled a new breed of start-ups. Though not the most successful of this bunch—his windfall from Red Swoosh hardly put him in the top tier of the richest dot-com entrepreneurs—Kalanick was one of its social ringleaders. He was a reliable presence at various conferences, often organizing impromptu "jam sessions" for like-minded people to kick around ideas. It was a group whose self-selecting members created, in their language, an "ecosystem" with a "positive feedback loop" of idea generation, creative riffing, and mutual self-promotion.

Some of those who hung out at Kalanick's JamPad when they were just starting out became the generation's leading lights. Aaron Levie, founder of a software company called Box.com, had met Kalanick in Los Angeles in 2005, while a student at the University of Southern California. Levie had sought out Mark Cuban, "because he was a famous blogger," to ask if he'd invest in Levie's dorm-room start-up, which used the Internet to store files once confined to computer hard drives. Cuban, who had recently invested in Red Swoosh, asked Kalanick to vet Levie for him. "We met at a café in LA," says Levie of Kalanick. "He was one of the first real entrepreneurs we met." Cuban invested in Levie's company, and the young entrepreneur dropped out of school and moved to Berkeley. He met up with Kalanick the first weekend he was in town. "He made you think harder than a lot of people. At that stage you don't get advice from billionaires only. I'd call him late at night, and he'd calm me down."

The JamPad became a focal point for San Francisco's up-and-coming entrepreneurs. Most were relative nobodies at the time. They were young and unestablished. Some had been at places like Google or Yahoo and were casting about for their next gig. In Kalanick they found a quirky kindred spirit, an engineer interested in start-ups for the sake of start-ups. Evan Williams, who sold his first company, Blogger, to Google and then started Twitter, hung out at Kalanick's house. So did Chris Sacca, a former lawyer who'd worked at Google and would become central to Uber's founding team and an early investor. (In 2016, Sacca became a cast member on the reality-television show *Shark Tank* alongside Mark Cuban, one of the show's stalwarts.) Shawn Fanning, Kalanick's friend who had flamed out at Napster, visited the JamPad too. The conversation, recalls Levie, "wasn't about working backward from an end state." Instead, it was taking an idea and spinning it forward, asking how it would be disruptive, who you were going to have to fight to succeed. "That's how our environment works."

Put differently, there was a purpose to the jam sessions at Kalanick's house. "The JamPad was less about getting all the smartest people in a room and sharing with each other," says Sacca, who got to know Kalanick because both had sold companies to Akamai. "It was more about: bring your company here, and we're going to work on what the future of the company should be." Kalanick's jam sessions were a movable feast. He'd often convene them at conferences like South by Southwest in Austin or LeWeb in Paris, frequently in rented homes he'd share with friends. Though some women participated, the jamming culture was unapologetically male, its core participants known in the tech press as "brogrammers." For one Consumer Electronics Show in Las Vegas, Kalanick bragged on Twitter about a rental he'd spotted: "In my Vegas pad quest, I found the ultimate pad, formally named the PIMP HOUSE, equipped with stripper pole AND stage." For good measure, he included a link to a photo.

The informal group mixed business with pleasure. Sacca often hosted Kalanick at his home near Lake Tahoe, where his hot tub became, inevitably, the JamTub. "Travis could spend hours and hours in that tub," recalls Sacca. As a houseguest, Kalanick was game for impromptu dance parties or late-night snowshoeing. At rest or not, Kalanick viewed it all as a form of work. Says Sacca: "Travis just wanted to talk and pace and do his thing where he's walking around, talking with his hands about ideas."

Kalanick made the most of his unemployed period, yet he approached leisure time more purposefully than the typical vagabond. He joined a group of entrepreneurs who called themselves the Random Travelers Society. The members literally spun a globe to choose a place to visit and then treated the adventure like a combination boondoggle/business fact-finding trip. "You want to dive into the region's culture, its business community and its education and government leadership," Kalanick explained in a 2009 blog post that described a trip the twelve-man group took to West Africa. Members of the group encouraged one another to research their business network before takeoff in order to arrange meetings on the road. In West Africa, Kalanick reported that the group met with the U.S. ambassadors to Portugal and Cape Verde as well as a "managing director at Senegal's largest bank."

Back home, he pursued the angel investing game slightly differently from others, often spending a considerable amount of time with each company in which he invested. He disliked the approach of other angels who treated small investments like so many chips on a roulette table. "I'm a heart entrepreneur," he says. "So there'd be a few companies that at any given time I'd be doing fifteen hours a week with. I was kind of like their CXO"—meaning a top-level jack-of-all-trades. He played such a role at Flowtown, a marketing software company in which prominent early-stage venture capitalist Steve Anderson had invested. "I like working with people who show up and do the work," says Anderson. "Travis was an ideal angel." Compared with what would become of UberCab, one of the companies in which he dabbled during this time, Kalanick's success rate was modest at best. Some of the companies he advised got bought, including Flowtown and DeviantArt. Others, like CrowdFlower, StyleSeat, Kareo, and Expensify, toiled in relative obscurity for years after Kalanick went back to work. Indeed, this partial list of Kalanick's pre-Uber investments shows just how random the start-up game can be. For every Twitter and Box there are oodles of Crowd-Flowers and Flowtowns. Even Kalanick couldn't predict—or will into existence—multiple successful start-up ventures.

What the dabbling and socializing did give Kalanick was an inside view of companies that might become his next full-time gig. For a while, he says he was too traumatized by his experiences with Scour and Red Swoosh to jump into the fray. "I was scared to do it again," he says. "I had this line back then, that money won't buy you happiness, but it will pay for therapy." He says he eventually found inspiration to return to work from Woody Allen, of all people. He says after watching Allen's 2008 film *Vicky Cristina Barcelona*, he marveled at the filmmaker's durability. "It was a great film, and I'm like, 'Woody Allen's in his seventies. This dude's been making movies for a long time, and he's still doing it.'" Translation: Kalanick was ready to be an entrepreneur again.

Still, he played his cards patiently. In 2010, Kalanick became deeply involved with a fast-growing questions-and-answers Web site called Formspring. The company's midwestern founders had recently relocated to California and got connected with Kalanick. "The whole Silicon Valley scene was new to them," says Anderson, the venture capitalist and a Formspring investor. Kalanick also invested in Formspring and began playing a more active role. "He was their coach." Kalanick seriously considered a bigger role at Formspring. "He was looking for something more than investing," says Anderson. "So we had a conversation around his running it. The numbers were exploding."

Though years later he'd downplay it, Kalanick was tempted by Formspring. Julie Supan, a marketing consultant who worked simultaneously with Formspring and another brand-new start-up, Airbnb, recalls Kalanick as more forceful than the average adviser. "He was dictatorial," she says. "He would walk into a room and he would stay standing as you sat. But he also was incredibly smart."

Coaching and advising allowed Kalanick to evaluate multiple companies simultaneously. Even as he was getting more deeply involved with Formspring, whose founders wanted him to be its CEO, he was hanging out with a friend from the start-up circuit named Garrett Camp. A soft-spoken Canadian engineer, Camp had founded and successfully sold a company called Stumble-Upon, built around an app for finding information on the Web. In 2010, Camp was ramping up one of his many ideas, a smart-phone app called UberCab that allowed a user to summon a lim-ousine in San Francisco. Kalanick was putting in time with UberCab just as he was with Formspring, which at the time showed far more impressive user growth.

In hindsight, the Uber-versus-Formspring decision seems obvious. It certainly was to Camp. "I was like, 'Dude, Formspring?' It had growth but how was it going to make money?" reflects Camp. "I told him there's going to be significant revenue at Uber."

Kalanick says it wasn't so much UberCab's potential revenue that made him take the plunge. Instead, he describes the chal-lenge in language that evokes a jigsaw puzzle, a particularly tough one that might come together in a beautiful picture. "I started see-ing a few things," he says. "First, it was super complex. And by com-plexity it's like there was so much uncertainty in all the pieces, especially because there's so many variables involved. Second, it was super disruptive. And the third one was that math moves the needle. And the final piece was where I saw that this is not a limo company. This is a logistics company. This is a technology company where math matters. That was the final slot for me. And it was just at the right time."

Once he knew it was the right time—it was September 2010—Kalanick moved quickly. "There was a moment when he just picked up and left Formspring," recalls Supan. Anderson was trying to persuade Kalanick to become Formspring's CEO. But it wasn't to be. In the fall of 2010, says Anderson, "he came to my office and said, 'I'm going to Uber.'"

CHAPTER 5
Early Days

U ber might never have happened if an amiable Canadian software designer named Garrett Camp hadn't pissed off San Francisco's two biggest taxi companies. It was the summer of 2008, and Camp, a native of Calgary who'd lived in the Bay Area for all of two years, had become weary of the cat-and-mouse game San Franciscans had grown used to playing with taxi dispatchers. It was often tough to hail a cab in the city, so most folks called to request a pickup. Camp had the numbers of two cab companies, Yellow and Luxor, stored on his phone. "Typically you'd call a cab and they'd say it would be there in fifteen to twenty minutes. It was kind of their standard response. But sometimes it would be thirty, or they wouldn't even show up," he says. Worse, he'd see empty cabs roll right by without stopping. "I think they were dispatching to a particular person and not necessarily the nearest cab, and so sometimes I would get frustrated and I would just get into the nearest one I saw. Then I'd get a call from the dispatcher saying, 'Where are you? We're here.' And I'd say, 'I already left because you guys were late.' That happened enough times that I got blacklisted. For a while neither company would pick up my calls."

This being San Francisco, Camp wasn't your average taxi passenger. It turned out he was the wrong guy to banish. The previous year he had sold his start-up, StumbleUpon, to eBay for $75 million, though he remained with eBay, running the company. StumbleUpon's offices were near South Park, a neighborhood near downtown that had been the epicenter for Internet companies during the industry boom of the late 1990s. Camp, who began calling pricier but more reliable limousine services in addition to hailing cabs when possible, hit on a solution to his problem. The fix capitalized on a shift in the business strategy of an iconic Silicon Valley company that was on the cusp of stratospheric growth.

In 2007, the same year Camp became a multimillionaire, Apple released the first iPhone. Though heralded as a breakthrough product for its revolutionary touchscreen, the product that would transform Apple got off to a slow start. In the United States, its first market, it worked only on AT&T's network, known for spotty service. And the phone's only "apps," software programs that enabled noncalling options like surfing the Web or managing a calendar, were installed on the phone by Apple. Outside software developers worked so hard to create unauthorized apps for the iPhone, however, that in 2008 Apple reversed course. Seizing both a business opportunity and a way to enhance the value of the phone, Apple created a mobile shopping site, the App

Store, that allowed any developer to create a program for the iPhone, provided it first received Apple's approval.

That summer, Camp was standing at the corner of Second and South Park streets with his iPhone in hand and running late for a date, when the proverbial lightbulb flicked on in his head. "I thought, 'Why can't I just request a car from my phone?'" An engineer, he knew the iPhone included a GPS chip, a semiconductor that could transmit its location to a network of satellites. "So I thought, 'Okay, if you put one iPhone in the car and it has the GPS location, and you have one in your hand, then dispatchers don't have to take down addresses anymore. There could just be one button in the app that says, 'Pick me up.'"

Camp did some research and found some apps that did a version of what he was after. One, Taxi Magic, connected users to taxi dispatchers, but didn't offer the instant gratification he was after. It had, he says, an "old-school, Web 1.0 experience," the ultimate put-down in the dawning mobile age. What Camp understood was the technology that lurked inside the iPhone that presented another game-changing opportunity. It was called an accelerometer, a motion sensor that's standard in aircraft guidance systems and automobile airbags but was new to phones. The accelerometer would be key for fitness devices like Fitbit and later the Apple Watch, which could track steps traveled with great accuracy. Camp envisioned another possibility. Together with the GPS technology in the phone, the accelerometer meant it was possible to track not just where a car was but also how fast it was moving. With this information, a phone could "automate billing in the background," Camp says. In other words, while a taxi meter shows a price clicking by over the course of a ride, a system that used smartphones with chips in them could spit out an image of a map that showed the beginning and end of the trip as well as its duration. In addition, by harnessing the computing power in the phone, a central computer would link a rider with a driver—cutting out the dispatcher middleman altogether.

Camp began discussing his idea with friends, which was second nature to the young entrepreneurs of San Francisco. Then he did something most people wouldn't think to do but that had become part of Camp's entrepreneurial repertoire: On August 8, 2008, he paid $35 to reserve a Web site, www.ubercab .com. Years later, Uber's name would represent an overarching strategy of providing transportation services at a massive, global level. For some, the German *über* would constitute a kind of menace, evocative of Nietzsche's *Übermensch*. That had nothing to do with why Camp chose the name. For starters, his annoyance with taxis notwithstanding, Camp originally set out to improve the limousine provisioning experience, not the dismal state of finding a taxi. This was a problem bigger than he was considering at the time. Camp conceived of his limo on-demand service as a fleet of sleek Mercedes S-Class luxury sedans, not the boxier Lincoln Town Cars that were more common in San Francisco. "I envisioned it as a much more elegant, more efficient sort of system for getting around," he says. To Camp, *über* connoted German elegance for his "better cab system"—and a company name was born as no more than a placeholder.

Reserving a Web site was mere table stakes for Camp, a form of paying for squatting rights on a spot that might one day hold a business. In fact, he registered names all the time for companies he might want to build later. "Garrett loves to buy domain names," says Ryan Sarver, a friend of Camp's who was an executive at Twitter during Uber's formative years. "Whenever I have an idea I call up Garrett and he sends me to his guy to check out availability and cost."

Making a business of an idea, even one with a catchy name and its own Web site, would require far more effort. Having built and sold one company—for a price tag many times greater than Kalanick's exit—gave Camp the ideal building blocks to try.

Camp and some friends at the University of Calgary started StumbleUpon in 2001. It was a simple software product that involved installing a tab on a PC's toolbar—this was long before smartphones and their clever third-party apps existed—that helped a user find interesting things on the Web. With a simple thumbs-up or thumbs-down, StumbleUpon's algorithm would find other things someone might like to view. It was what Camp later would refer to as a Web 1.0 experience. Still, the simplicity of the product masked the complexity of the software code necessary to build it. Camp was getting a master's degree in software engineering, and though he and his friends bootstrapped StumbleUpon with their labor and little cash, their graduate research dovetailed with the product. Camp's thesis was on "information retrieval through collaborative interface design and evolutionary algorithms."

Like Facebook, which began a few years later, StumbleUpon was a dorm-room success. It grew quickly to hundreds of thousands of users with Camp and his cofounders as the only employees. (Revenue would follow in later years with an early form of "native" advertising, full-page ads that would appear after several "stumbles," or items users were discovering.) As he was nearing the completion of his degree, in 2005, Camp visited the San Francisco Bay Area, partly because Geoff Smith, a Stumble-Upon cofounder, was attending a conference hosted by Singularity University, a group that explores a future where humans and machines unite. On that trip and another later in the year, Camp met several investors—including prominent angel investors Josh Kopelman, Ram Shriram, Brad O'Neill, and Ron Conway—who were eager to buy stakes in StumbleUpon based on its multitude of users.

The Canadians were amazed at how easy it was to raise money in California. Reflects Camp: "Everyone's like, 'So how many employees do you have?' We didn't have any employees. 'And how much money have you raised?' Nothing. 'And who else is helping?' Just us." Camp says he had no burning desire to move to California following graduate school—Vancouver, London, and Montreal were also on his wish list—but he was entranced by the heady atmosphere of investors who understood technology. "They got what I was trying to do," he says. "There's definitely a lot of tech in Calgary, but it's more wireless or oil and gas tech. There wasn't a lot of Web tech." San Francisco was different: "I just had these five meetings, and every single person said yes."

In short order Camp became part of the San Francisco start-up scene. In 2007, less than two years after first visiting the Bay Area to raise money, Camp sold StumbleUpon to eBay, which was attracted to the start-up's intuitive recommendation tool. That same year he attended a new conference called the Lobby.

Started by David Hornik, a venture capitalist with August Capital, the conference's conceit was that the best interactions at such events happen in the hallway, not onstage. The Lobby would cut to the chase and eliminate the typical presentations and panels—making the gathering strictly and unabashedly about networking. Hornik's audience would be transparently self-serving: all the entrepreneurs and would-be entrepreneurs he'd worked with in the past or might want to work with in the future. The Lobby gathered at the plush Fairmont Orchid on the Big Island of Hawaii, and it was the first time Camp met Travis Kalanick, whose company, Red Swoosh, had been in the portfolio of August Capital. Camp and Kalanick shared a dinner in Hawaii with Evan Williams, cofounder of Twitter, the buzziest new start-up in San Francisco at the time.

In the months after Camp reserved his UberCab Web site, in late 2008, he started to circulate his idea among his entrepreneurial social crowd. "It was really just a concept that I was bouncing off my friends to see what they thought," he says. "It was just kind of a mental exercise, and every time I would take a Town Car I would think a little bit more. And then I started interviewing drivers, and they told me that two thirds of the time they were just sitting idle. I thought if the cost came down and drivers did five times as many short trips per day instead of just trips to the airport, that it would get to the price point where people would probably use it more like they use a cab."

In hindsight, the founding of what became Uber seems like

it must have been an important moment. At the time, it amounted to little more than a "jamming" exercise, one that might lead to something interesting but more likely wouldn't. "I was looking for friends that could be my advisers," says Camp, "and I sort of had my first four friends who expressed interest become my advisers. Travis was one of them." The others were Tim Ferriss, who had recently released a book, *The 4-Hour Workweek*, which launched him on a lucrative pop-culture career as a noted author, speaker, and podcast host; Steve Jang, a friend with modest start-up successes under his belt; and Steve Russell, who had invested in StumbleUpon. Indeed, Uber got going mostly in Camp's head and as a conversation piece among friends. "I kind of bounced the idea off a bunch of people and they were the ones who kind of thought it was interesting. It was pretty casual. I had some mock-ups. And the concept was coming together. I was spending a lot of time doing research online."

The early days of Uber were so casual that it had no office or employees. But the more Camp talked about it the more people got involved. Oscar Salazar, a classmate from the University of Calgary who had moved to New York, agreed to do some coding for Camp's prototypes. Salazar in turn recruited some of his friends in Mexico to work on UberCab's Web site. In San Francisco, one of Camp's pals was particularly helpful, both for his idea generation and for hosting jam sessions at his home. Says Camp: "Travis was the best brainstorming partner."

The limo-hailing idea interested Camp, Kalanick, and the others, but it was hardly the only thing any of them were working on. Camp, after all, worked for eBay, and Kalanick was still at Akamai. But neither was in the kind of role that demanded all their attention. Life inside the big companies that acquired them allowed for plenty of time to work on their "side hustles" and also to hang out with each other. In early December 2008, the duo traveled to Paris for another industry conference, this one created by Loïc Le Meur, a French blogger who yearned to break into the ranks of Silicon Valley entrepreneurs. Together with his wife at the time, Géraldine, he succeeded in attracting a group of many of the best young Internet personalities from the United States, who needed little arm-twisting to join a boondoggle in Paris. For European attendees, LeWeb was an opportunity to rub shoulders with Silicon Valley's up-and-coming elite.

Le Meur, who ran the conference for twelve years, recounts with pride the significant moments that happened in Paris. "Jack Dorsey," a cofounder of Twitter, "launched Square at LeWeb," he brags. "SoundCloud found funding from Fred Wilson at LeWeb," he says, referring to a popular European music-storing service and a prominent New York–based venture capitalist, respectively. And referring to an Israeli mapping company that later would be bought by Google and form the foundation of Google's competition with Uber: "Waze won our start-up competition." The techies even experienced romance in the city of love. "Marissa got engaged at LeWeb," says Le Meur, namechecking Marissa Mayer, the Google executive who became CEO of Yahoo. Her then boyfriend, Zachary Bogue, asked Le Meur where would be a good place in Paris to propose. "I said: 'Onstage.' He refused."

The LeWeb conference of 2008 was memorable not for what happened onstage but for the blizzard that slammed Paris while it was happening. Le Meur struggled to get his speakers and attendees to the convention hall in the snow. Parisian taxi drivers, already held in low esteem by many, didn't help matters. "They wouldn't say hello, they'd object to a short ride, they were unwilling to give you change," says Le Meur, a native of Perpignan, a small city in southern France, near the Spanish border. And then, when the snowstorm hit, "the taxis went home. You couldn't find any. It was very inspiring for Garrett and Travis."

In fact, Camp in particular needed little inspiration, as he'd already been mulling a solution to surly taxi drivers, in another city, for months. The blizzard did, however, provide the pair an opportunity to tromp off to the Eiffel Tower, where they climbed the stairs and rode the elevator to the top and talked more about Camp's UberCab idea. The conversation became part of the lore of the company's founding, the moment the two decided to start a company. It is a convenient story, particularly for Kalanick, who wasn't present at the creation of UberCab. Uber's corporate Web site, in a section labeled "Our Story," would say that "on a snowy Paris evening in 2008, Travis Kalanick and Garrett Camp had trouble hailing a cab. So they came up with a simple idea—tap a button, get a ride." Like other company creation myths, it was an elegant, if oversimplified, yarn of an aha moment that didn't quite tell the whole story.

What did happen that night, says Camp, was that Kalanick contributed a key insight that eventually would make a difference between a so-so start-up "jam" and what became Uber. At the time, Camp was convinced, as he would be for some time, that he wanted to be in the business of owning limos and employing drivers. He even contemplated leasing a garage. Kalanick dissuaded him. "Travis was trying to convince me on the Eiffel Tower, 'You don't need to buy cars. You can just give the app to drivers and let them be free agents. It's just a better model to have free agents working when they want to work, having full flexibility.'"

It was only later that Kalanick recognized the similarity between his high-level advice for Camp—leverage other people's labor and property rather than buying it yourself—and his earlier start-up experiences at Scour and Red Swoosh. "I didn't realize it at the time," he says, that "it's sort of the physical-world equivalent of where I came from. But your mind just finds these things."

Moreover, disrupting the transportation business wasn't the only concept on his mind that winter. "I had this one idea, that was basically a more buttoned-up corporate version of Airbnb. It was like long-term leases in all these places that had the same consistency everywhere but you had a home experience when you traveled. It was called Pad Pass." Kalanick's Twitter feed reveals other ideas he was noodling on while discussing limos with Camp. In December 2008, he broadcast that he was advising a company in the medical transcription business. Another project involved an art rental idea. "Everybody wants art in their lives, but nobody likes to buy it," he opined. "Who's down for a subscription rotating art collection? Low budget, high culture."

By early 2009, Camp and Kalanick had become committed traveling buddies. Chris Sacca, a frequent visitor to the JamPad, had been a "packager" for Barack Obama's presidential campaign. He raised $600,000 for the inauguration, and so he invited a large number of his posse—at $12,500 a pop—to attend a multiday party that would include the main event itself, a ball, and concerts by Beyoncé and Bruce Springsteen. Camp and Kalanick went together, joining a group that included Evan Williams as well as Tony Hsieh and Alfred Lin, both early investors in the online shoe retailer Zappos.

Once again, cold and wet weather bedeviled—and possibly inspired—the pair. "Travis and Garrett were fidgety and annoyed at waiting for cabs to get from party to party," recalls Lin. Experienced traveler though he'd become, Kalanick arrived in Washington unprepared. "We went to the inauguration concert together, and poor Travis had not properly packed for the chilly D.C. weather," says Lin's wife, Rebecca. "My memory is of Travis wearing one of those Peruvian knitted hats with the long side tassels and pompoms on top, which he had borrowed from his girlfriend at the time."

Back in San Francisco, Camp was beginning to think about his UberCab idea as something that had legs. But the idea took hold slowly. "I have ideas all the time," he says. "But you've got to usually come back to an idea repeatedly before you actually do something about it. And this was one that when you just want to stop thinking about it after a certain period of time you realize you've got to do something.

"I didn't really set out to start a company. It was more like I set out to create a product. But it was the only one I acted upon at the time." In the early part of 2009 Camp set up a bank account with $15,000 to fund the Web site he'd already begun to develop: Ubercab.com. Camp estimates that over its first eighteen months he funneled about $250,000 into UberCab.

Because Camp continued to divide his time with Stumble-Upon, the process would take most of the year, moving forward in fits and starts. "I came up with the interaction design and the flow for how it should work," he says. "I had mock-ups of how the flow would look. You would press a button and then you'd see the car accept and you'd see the driver rating. I'd done rating systems with StumbleUpon so I thought we should have a rating system here too. But instead of thumbs-up/thumbs-down, I thought that a star rating would probably be better because it would be a little bit higher resolution."

Initially, UberCab existed only on the Web. Its progression to full-fledged iPhone app was a multinational affair. Salazar, Camp's grad-school buddy from Calgary, already had farmed out some Web site work to developers in Mexico. Then he found two Dutchmen to design the young company's first app that would work on Apple's smartphone platform, called iOS.

As things gelled, Camp persuaded Kalanick to take a more active role in UberCab. Kalanick signed on as an adviser, but an active one with a big stake in the fledgling company's success. "He gave me like ten percent of the company," says Kalanick. "I spent a lot of time with the original engineering dudes." Toward the end of the year Camp was itching to give UberCab a try, but the software wasn't quite ready. Kalanick hired a software engineering firm called Mob.ly, which later would become the smartphone development team of the commerce site Groupon, to overhaul the iPhone app. Says Camp: "They basically rewrote the iOS app from the ground up and made it much more solid and stable."

With the rewritten app nearing completion, Camp and Kalanick began thinking about going for a test drive in the new year. Meantime, Camp continued his "research" by taking slick-looking sedans around town. Rob Hayes, a venture capitalist with First Round Capital, whose founder Josh Kopelman had invested in StumbleUpon, memorably spotted Camp riding in style on the 2009 holiday party circuit. "Every year Ram Shriram"—another investor who had staked Camp's first company—"has his Christmas party at his place in Woodside," a tony suburb near Palo Alto. "I remember Garrett showing up, I think with his date, in a black car and thinking, 'That's pretty cool. I drove here and he shows up in a black car,'" says Hayes. "I remember that kind of sticking with me." It would prove to be a lucrative observation.

⊙────────────────────────────────────⊙

Come January 2010, Camp and Kalanick, still dabbling part time on UberCab, were ready to begin testing the service. They also began making plans to launch operations in San Francisco, and they'd need someone to oversee it. On January 4, 2010, Kalanick posted a message on Twitter saying he was "looking 4 entrepreneurial product mgr/biz-dev killer 4 a location service." He went on, in a total of fewer than 140 characters, to note that the service was "pre-launch," that the right candidate would receive a "BIG" equity package, and that there were "big peeps involved," presumably referring to himself and Camp.

Among those who responded was a twenty-seven-year-old in Chicago working in a mid-level management job for General Electric named Ryan Graves, who desperately wanted to rebrand himself as a start-up guy. Graves had been active on the location "check-in" service Foursquare, going so far as to earn the rank of "mayor" of several Chicago neighborhoods—a distinction achieved by heavy usage. He had flown to New York unannounced to ask, unsuccessfully, for a job from Foursquare founder

Dennis Crowley. When Kalanick tweeted his request for tips for someone who might want the job of running Uber's launch in San Francisco, Graves responded on Twitter in three minutes: "here's a tip. Email me :)"

Soon after, Camp and Kalanick traveled to New York, along with Yishai Lerner, whose firm, Mob.ly, had redesigned UberCab's smartphone app. There they met Oscar Salazar, and they arranged for three limo drivers to test the app over the course of a couple wintry days. They also invited Graves to meet them for a job interview and a demo. "We just tried it a bunch of times," says Camp. Sometimes the app worked and other times it didn't. "We took a lot of notes." Kalanick met with Graves and hired him on the spot. The shot at his start-up dream secured, Graves and his wife, Molly, a kindergarten teacher, made plans to move to San Francisco, where he'd start at UberCab on March 1.

Just as Kalanick relied on Twitter to recruit UberCab's first businessperson, Camp tapped his Canadian software network to identify its first engineer. Conrad Whelan had taken a break from working at a technology company in Calgary during the early part of 2010 to travel across Europe. When he got back he contacted Camp to catch up. Camp asked his vagabond friend to join UberCab. "When I joined the company, you couldn't actually sign up for the product," remembers Whelan. "It was just a way to order the car. So I built the sign-up flows that would take a credit card and make user accounts."

The young company immediately embraced a start-up cliché: the cramped office space. UberCab's few employees jammed into a conference room lent to them by another start-up, a travel site called Zozi. Ryan McKillen, who knew Graves at Miami

University in Ohio, joined Uber as a software engineer shortly after Whelan. His first unexpected obstacle was a language barrier. "On the morning of my first day I remember noticing this stack of books on the table," says McKillen. "All these computer science books, programming, databases, all this stuff. They're pristine—the bindings on the books had never been broken. And there's this one tattered book on the table that looks like it's gotten all kinds of love, a lot of use. And so, the first thing I say is, 'Hey, Conrad, why is there a Spanish-to-English dictionary on the table?' And he looks back up at me and goes, 'Well, Ryan, because the code is written in Spanish. Welcome to Uber.'" (The Spanish code in question was thanks to the Mexican developers Oscar Salazar had hired.)

As the engineers beefed up UberCab's code, Graves began visiting garages in San Francisco to sign up drivers. This task required persistence and patience, particularly when explaining how to use a prototype smartphone app in lieu of a dispatch service. Graves cut a formidable figure. A six-five Midwesterner with a firm handshake and a broad smile, Graves "looks like he's in a 1960s cigarette ad," says Chris Sacca, part of the UberCab advisory crew at the time. "Ryan is a hustle guy. He knows how to walk into a garage full of suspicious Armenian cab drivers and come out with hugs."

In late May 2010, Uber launched quietly, with just a handful of drivers and customers in San Francisco, the latter coming primarily from the new version of word of mouth: "followers" of Kalanick, Camp, and a few others on Twitter. Compared with a big-company launch, like a new iPhone, for example, the debut of

UberCab was low-key. If you weren't on Twitter you wouldn't know about it. There was a small group of people in San Francisco who were aware of such things, sort of like the in-the-know types who somehow divine the latest pop-up restaurants and bars. In fact, from the beginning, Uber positioned itself as a toy built for its young-men-about-town founders, as embodied by its initial marketing slogan: "Everyone's Private Driver." The frugal Kalanick—a cheapskate well after becoming a paper billionaire—credits Camp as the inspiration for Uber as a lifestyle. "There's nobody that's got more swagger getting into or out of an Uber than Garrett Camp," says Kalanick.

Within days of launching UberCab, Kalanick, who had taken the title "chief incubator," and Graves began raising money for the new business. A start-up asking for money needed a CEO, and so Graves, hired as general manager after tweeting Kalanick for a job, got the title. "You can't do a seed round without having a CEO," says Kalanick, who was involved only part time in Uber. "Graves was in it full time, so we're like, 'Graves, you're CEO.'"

The two tag-teamed investor pitches, which initially didn't go well. August Capital's David Hornik didn't like the idea, he says, because he didn't think the livery business was big enough. Bill Gurley at Benchmark Capital had similar reservations. Ram Shriram, who'd made money with Camp on StumbleUpon, felt UberCab didn't have the right attributes for a technology company. "I told them, 'I don't invest in capital-intensive businesses, and I don't want to end up with fifteen Lincoln Town Cars in my driveway.'" Numerous investors saw a red flag in Camp and

Kalanick's reluctance to join UberCab full time. And Ryan Graves, three months into his Silicon Valley entrepreneurial career, wasn't a satisfactory CEO.

One investor who saw UberCab's potential was Rob Hayes of First Round Capital. Hayes had been following Camp on Twitter and noticed his periodic references to "UberCab," though Hayes, a decade older and not a member of the same social scene, had no idea what it was. On June 15, 2010, when the new service had been running for just a few weeks, Hayes sent Camp an e-mail titled "UberCab." The e-mail read, in its entirety: "I'll bite :-) Can I learn more?" Camp quickly put Hayes together with Graves, who pitched him on the investment. "I tried the product once, and it was a good experience," says Hayes. "It made sense to me as a San Franciscan who had totally given up on taxis that this was going to work here and would likely work in other places." Other VCs pooh-poohed UberCab because of the limited potential for a limo service. Hayes says he was enthralled not by limos but by how convenient UberCab was to use. "I knew that using the existing black-car market as a proxy for how big this could get was wrong. Beyond that I had no idea about Uber and UberX. I wasn't even sure New York would work. But I knew it was better than what was here today and that it solved a real customer problem."

The entire "seed" round for UberCab's first investment, led by First Round and also including Chris Sacca's fund, Lowercase Capital, and a smattering of San Francisco angel investors, was $1.25 million and valued Uber at $4 million, not including the new money. Just a few years later such an amount would prove to be less than a rounding error for Uber. First Round, a firm that invests only in seed rounds, wrote a check for $450,000. The bet would net the firm billions in return.

Money in hand, Kalanick had finally concluded that it was time to go to work for UberCab, which had moved into the offices of First Round Capital, in San Francisco's South of Market neighborhood. There was only one job that interested Kalanick, however, and Ryan Graves was doing it. Working through Sacca as an intermediary, Kalanick orchestrated a demotion for Graves, to vice president of operations and general manager for San Francisco. (As a lawyer, board member, investor, and friend to the founders, Sacca was well positioned to play go-between in the still highly informal company.) Kalanick also wanted a bigger piece of UberCab than the 10 percent stake Camp had given him originally. He demanded 23 percent, with part of the shares coming from Camp and Graves. Camp says he already had learned the value of giving up equity to sign key hires. "I was very willing to give good amounts to get the right people," he says. As for Graves, he told the technology news site *TechCrunch* that he was "super pumped" Kalanick was joining Uber full time, a comment the snarky site mocked in its headline given Graves's demotion. Despite his hurt feelings and subsequent feuds with Kalanick over his right to be called a founder, Graves stayed with Uber in senior positions, and on its board, for years. He also coined a phrase that's central to the Uber culture. Years later Uber employees continued to say, without a whiff of irony, that they were "super pumped" about just about anything.

On the day Kalanick became CEO, in October 2010, a man carrying a clipboard showed up at UberCab's offices looking for Ryan Graves. He brought a cease-and-desist letter from the San Francisco Metro Transit Authority and California Public Utilities Commission. "The name UberCab indicates that you are a taxicab company or affiliated with a taxicab company, and as such you are under the jurisdiction of the SFMTA," it read. Kalanick's response was straightforward. The company would drop the word "cab" from its name and otherwise ignore the letter.

CHAPTER 6
Travis Takes the Wheel

T he company Travis Kalanick decided to take over in the fall of 2010 was still tiny. It had been operating in a single city, San Francisco, for four months. For the entire month of September, when Kalanick negotiated his terms for becoming CEO, UberCab transported 427 riders. As it would raise money and expand to a handful of additional cities over the course of the next year, the young company would be fueled by a combination of transformative technology and old-fashioned, seat-of-the-pants human effort. Uber's was a "hustle culture," with a can-do spirit of long hours and a try-anything-once work ethic. In time, Kalanick would hit on the trope of "bits and atoms" to describe Uber's unique matching of digital prowess with physical assets that set it apart from the prominent Internet companies that had come before it.

Such pithy descriptions were a ways off, however. At the time, Kalanick saw Uber as a math problem in need of solving, math being a favorite metaphor of his to describe complicated operational challenges.

If Kalanick was visualizing equations in the ether, like Russell Crowe's John Nash character in the film *A Beautiful Mind*, Uber's earliest employees were preoccupied in the months before his full-time arrival with far more mundane aspects of creating a new enterprise. Austin Geidt was one of Uber's original employees, hired as an office intern in the summer of 2010. Just twenty-five years old, Geidt was a former English major who had gotten a slow start to her career. (Half a decade later, when she was one of Uber's most senior executives, Geidt would tell her story of resiliency, having overcome drug addiction before joining Uber. The stresses of working at a hypergrowth company in the spotlight, she would say, were manageable compared with what she'd already overcome.) Like many others, Geidt's introduction to Uber came via Twitter. "I was looking for jobs, and it was a bad economy," she recounts. "I was following random tech people on Twitter, and I saw some tweets about Uber, and it looked interesting. I heard they were looking for an intern, and so I reached out to Ryan Graves, who was CEO at the time, and told him, 'You've got to give me a shot.'" He did.

As one of the few nonengineers on the small staff, Geidt became the go-to person for logistical tasks large and small. She was part office manager, part market researcher, and part customer-service agent. Geidt cold-called limo drivers she found on the consumer recommendations Web site Yelp to ask if they wanted to drive for Uber. She handed out "flyers that no one wanted" at San Francisco's Yerba Buena convention center. The only phone number posted on Uber's Web site and its app connected directly to her cell phone. "I would get calls at three A.M., saying, 'I can't get a car,' or 'Hey, I need a car at Fourth and whatever.' And I'd say, 'You're going to have to use the app.' So we shut down that number." Geidt gained valuable insight into the vagaries of start-up life. "I didn't know how to write a proper e-mail," she says. "And then I quickly learned, oh, everyone's kind of making this up. In a start-up, no one knows what they're doing."

This start-up made plenty of mistakes. During its first months of operating in San Francisco, in the middle of 2010, it was run by a first-time CEO, Ryan Graves, while Camp and Kalanick continued to dabble elsewhere. Many of these snafus and on-the-job training led directly to what would become the Uber "playbook." Its first Halloween, for example, Uber offered discounts to riders as a way to drum up business. The discounts worked too well, resulting in unhappy customers. "No one could get a car," says Geidt, noting that the promotion had generated demand unmatched by the supply of available drivers. "And so we learned that you don't give a discount on your highest-demand day. We just didn't know." (Indeed, in time Uber would take the opposite approach: it would raise prices at busy times, a hated and controversial tactic called surge pricing that nevertheless had the desired effect of encouraging more drivers to take to the streets.)

Geidt wasn't the only one learning as she went. Graves began visiting garages belonging to owners of limo fleets. He was focused exclusively on livery drivers, not cabbies, and Graves found himself evangelizing to chauffeurs whose technological acumen wasn't high. "It was this pitch where I had an iPad, so it was visible from a presentation perspective. And I had to show both experiences," he says, referring to how customers would request rides and how drivers would accept them. "It was a big Google map with a big green button and the address that the pin in the middle was over. That's it. I'd hit the green button in a live demo and hope it worked." Smartphones were such a pricey novelty at the time that Uber decided to distribute a dedicated iPhone, free of charge, to all drivers. "We did a deal with AT&T super early," says Graves, referring to the large carrier known for erratic wireless coverage but at the time the exclusive U.S. distributor of the iPhone. "I think I opened the largest private, nongovernment AT&T account in their history. We had a few hundred thousand phones at some point."

Holidays would prove to be significant inflection points for Uber, for both good and ill, during that first year of operations. Rob Hayes, the seed-round investor from First Round Capital, had a bird's-eye view of Uber's early development. For several months in late 2010 the company had moved into his firm's offices in San Francisco's South of Market neighborhood. Kalanick's desk was nearby, and the two spoke frequently. "Growth was just torrid those first few months," says Hayes. "And then Thanksgiving happened, and growth fell off a cliff. Travis had this chart that showed growth in rides. And there was this huge dip for the whole week of Thanksgiving. And it was like: 'Oh shit, what happened? Is it not working anymore?'" In fact, Uber hadn't stopped working. It was just that its youthful customers were off somewhere, likely wherever they grew up, not out on the town partying. "The week after Thanksgiving it went right back up to where it had been if you continued on that exponential curve. And then

New Year's hit. And it blew away all our expectations. It was just crazy."

Word of mouth accounted for Uber's early popularity with customers, but generating supply—signing up drivers to satisfy rider demand—required a different approach. Limo drivers, after all, didn't have the same social-media habits as twentysomething-year-old software coders; they were not scouring Twitter to know about the latest tech start-ups. Only licensed drivers were eligible to drive for Uber, and all had existing customers of their own. No matter how successful Ryan Graves was in wooing them, the drivers would never pledge exclusivity to Uber. Yet if ever a holiday was built for Uber, it was the drunken revelry of New Year's Eve. Graves manned a desk at Uber's offices on that last day of 2010, signing up drivers and handing out iPhones preloaded with the Uber driver app. "We were at it literally until almost eleven P.M. on New Year's Eve," he says. "It was like, 'How many guys can I get in this door and show them how the application works and give them a device, get their account all set up, and get them on the road for tonight?' Because every extra driver we could add was going to help make the experience better for our riders and the supply would be better and the market would work better. It was a grind to the very last minute."

Having begun to gain traction in San Francisco, in 2011 Uber started replicating itself in other cities. Its expansion plan initially focused on market size and the perceived tech savvy of a local market. At least at the outset, the thinking was that cities with a multitude of tech professionals would provide a leg up in proselytizing the new service and help a team visiting from San Francisco to make the connections necessary to get going. New York was Uber's first new city, a large market but also one that, unlike San Francisco, had a robust taxi industry. In rapid succession Uber would also turn on its app in Seattle, Chicago, Boston, and Washington, D.C.

Ryan Graves, now head of "operations," oversaw each new city launch and the general managers hired to run them. Austin Geidt, his deputy and former intern, was in charge of developing a process for starting operations wherever Uber went. She helped out in New York but had her first big test in Seattle. Her orders were to pack a bag and fly north in preparation for a launch that would be months away. Once again, Geidt was learning on the go. Her guidance from Kalanick was to treat a city launch the way his old Random Travelers Society approached a foreign adventure. "We tried to get into the tech world to make sure that we got to a lot of Travis's contacts ahead of time," she says. The approach was unique. Uber needed to have relationships with drivers and government officials, sure. But by promoting first in the tech world it could generate buzz and attract cutting-edge users, just as it had in San Francisco. "We talked to people at Amazon and Microsoft, for example. I met the community manager at Yelp and his photographer friend. It was kind of all over the place. It was just about getting me plugged in to Seattle. The tech community really took care of me when I was launching."

Geidt worked backward from the endgame of offering rides

to the public. First, there were regulatory concerns to consider, and she would start with a visit to City Hall to obtain the pertinent regulations. "I would go through every single clause of the regs and try and piece together where we could have a problem." A normal company would have arranged meetings with regulators to signal their intentions; Uber approached each launch like a guerilla attack, with no need to warn the enemy first. Operational building blocks came next. "I'm going to need to get a ton of partners," says Geidt, using Uberspeak for drivers. "I'm going to have to sell them on this app. I'm going to have to design the pricing." She would plan parties for drivers and local influencers, reach out to the press, and finally, plan a launch date.

Geidt recognized that the steps she was taking were repeatable. "I took notes on everything I was doing as I was launching the city, which kind of became a very sloppy version of our first playbook," she says. "And then each city I would go to thereafter, I would try to refine how to make this more efficient and streamline this process." After the Seattle launch, Geidt took her notes to the next city. "When I went to Boston afterwards, it was a matter of tightening it up." For the next five years Geidt would run the growing team that oversaw market introductions around the world, following the same playbook she developed for Uber in the summer of 2011: assess regulations, recruit drivers, develop pricing, woo local media and celebrities, and so on.

In its earliest days, Uber was masterful with local public relations. It would announce its presence with a blog post, often from Kalanick, declaring its love for the city in which it was launching. Kalanick would highlight a city's key attributes, whether it was its sports teams or dominant industry. "Geeks run the show here in Seattle," he announced in August 2011; "35 years of Microsoft, 15 with Amazon, and many decades of Boeing have made Seattle a gadget, tech, app geek haven. Living in the future is a way of life. Pushing a button and within minutes having a shiny towncar arrive fits that mold." Kalanick cast himself and his colleagues from headquarters as amateur anthropologists, out to understand each new locale. "Celebrate the city" would become one of the company's written-down core values.

Adding local flavor to a rigorous playbook was an adaptation of Intel's famous "Copy Exactly" approach to manufacturing semiconductors, which itself was borrowed from the McDonald's technique of precisely replicating the taste of a Big Mac around the world. Internally, Uber would follow a rigid process for setting up shop in new cities, learning best practices as it went. It would use the same steps, the same language, the same metrics, for example, of how many employees to add on the ground as a ratio of trip activity. For external consumption, it would make an effort to feel as "local" as possible, including giving newly hired managers authority to tweak marketing language and decide what kind of publicity events would attract drivers and passengers.

Local media typically would fawn over the new service and its magical app. First-person accounts in local papers and Web sites frequently would detail the joys of summoning a car without a phone call and also exiting without fumbling for one's wallet or having to sign a credit card slip. Uber even led passengers to believe the tip was included, which most customers loved for the reduced friction in the experience. Uber also cleverly chose prominent locals to announce its arrival in town. Early cities experienced "viral" growth, the Holy Grail of Internet start-up development. To jump-start that virality, the company would designate a hometown celebrity as its "Rider Zero." The label, says Geidt, was a "positive take on 'patient zero,' the first early adopter to help our service spread like wildfire in a new city." Early examples of those chosen to hold the distinction of "rider zero" included local tech CEOs, sports stars, and other influential personalities. In Los Angeles, in early 2012, Travis Kalanick's parents were joint Rider Zero; the actor Edward Norton, an Uber investor and ardent celebrity cheerleader for the company, was Rider One.

For all the external whimsy, in time Uber would be known as one of the most grueling work environments in the technology industry. It attracted a certain type of employee, self-described growth junkies who valued the rigors of start-up life more than the pleasures of work-life balance. The company even found a way to get its employees to work while on vacation by institutionalizing Kalanick's maneuver at Red Swoosh of relocating the company to a Thai beach to code software in their flip-flops. At Uber, such jaunts became known as a "workation." Austin Geidt recalls one such trip, as Uber was slated to launch service in Melbourne, Australia, at the beginning of 2013. "We flew out a bunch of people from San Francisco for New Year's Eve of 2012," she says. It was when it first occurred to her that Uber was going to be something big. "Pretty much everyone in the company was on call. It's a really big day for us, and we were all on video with one another, and everyone was staying up all night. It was a goose bumps moment for me of like, 'Wow, we're a part of something really cool. Everyone has totally bought into this.'"

The growing business required additional capital to expand, and by early 2011 attracting it was relatively easy. Buzz was developing around Uber and its easy-to-use app. As a purveyor of rides in luxury sedans billing itself as "Everyone's Private Driver," Uber also had a unique advantage: the correlation between its core customer and potential investor was unusually high. (Uber cars didn't conform at the time to one make or model, but all were driven by licensed livery drivers. So the vast majority were Lincoln Town Cars and similar models that catered to business executives and other privileged types.) Bill Gurley, a venture capitalist with the venerable Menlo Park firm Benchmark Capital, says his partnership had rejected Uber during its seed round in 2010, having judged Ryan Graves too inexperienced a CEO to back. Matt Cohler, one of Benchmark's newer and younger partners, lived in San Francisco, and he became what Gurley calls a "power user" of Uber. "He started saying, 'This is the most valuable app on my phone,'" says Gurley. "He would say that over and over again: 'If I could only have one app on my phone, it would be this.'"

Travis Kalanick was more prepared than most entrepreneurs to raise money. After all, he had learned the craft under far less advantageous circumstances, having scraped together funding for Scour and Red Swoosh. "I had had to get very, very good at it because we had something that wasn't very compelling," he says. "When it's hard you have to be perfect." He also had gained more recent perspective in his brief "angel" investing career, learning the game from the other side of the table.

In fact, Kalanick had fashioned himself as a scholar of the art of the VC deal. In 2009, during his hiatus from full-time employment, he'd written a blog post for fellow entrepreneurs listing his fifteen "essential" fund-raising tips. Much of his advice was commonsense start-up pabulum, like how to generate excitement for one's deal, the importance of soliciting referrals, and how to "always be closing." Prosaic or not, Kalanick had worked out a method, and he intended to follow it while raising money for Uber. "Every communication you have with prospective investors must include a sense of momentum and urgency in the deal process," he wrote, adding helpful lines an entrepreneur could e-mail as follow-ups, like "Things are moving quickly" and "Many parties are interested."

Like many seasoned entrepreneurs, Kalanick liked to think of venture capitalists as necessary evils who would take advantage of start-ups if they could. He'd cynically turn the tables on the VCs if possible. "I knew how to create scarcity," he says. "I knew how to pack it all into one thing. I've had so much of my time wasted with VCs. I mean, I did hundreds and hundreds of VC meetings and raised a million bucks total." Now he relished his newfound leverage: investors wanted to give him money without his persuading them. What's more, he wanted them to name their price rather than the other way around. "Travis is great at creating demand," says Chris Sacca, the early Uber adviser and investor. "He says, 'I don't want to hear from you until this date. And on this date I'll ask you for terms, and I want you to tell me your terms. Then I'll come see you.'"

Benchmark Capital was ready to give Kalanick its terms. The firm had successfully invested in Internet "marketplaces" like eBay and OpenTable, and it saw Uber as a potential successor. "We had an internal thesis that other industries might benefit from a network layer on top of them," says Benchmark's Gurley. "And as we started discussing it, one of the things we thought about was transportation." Benchmark concluded that the taxi industry was a bad bet because of its arcane rules, fixed pricing, and concentrated ownership. "We literally had come to the conclusion internally that the minute we see an entrepreneur that tries to do this against black cars instead of taxis, we'd have an interest." Uber, of course, would in short order challenge the "arcane rules" that worried Gurley. But by initially co-opting the limousine market rather than cabs, it was attractive to Benchmark.

Kalanick met with multiple firms, including the full partnerships of Sequoia and Benchmark on the same day. Benchmark offered to invest and to put Matt Cohler, its partner who'd been such an enthusiastic supporter of Uber, on its board. Kalanick wanted Benchmark's money but not the partner who had championed the deal. "Matt Cohler had just become a VC," he recalls. "The idea of somebody experimenting their VC style on you is not something I was cool with." He preferred Gurley, a former Wall Street analyst who was a decade older than Kalanick and had been a VC far longer than Cohler. "It's like the devil-you-know kind of thing. At least I knew how this dude rolls." In February 2011, Benchmark invested $10 million in what was known as Uber's "A round," or its first full-fledged infusion of venture capital. Benchmark became the largest investor in Uber, and Gurley joined its board. Excluding the cash Benchmark agreed to commit, the investment valued Uber at $60 million.

By late 2011, Kalanick was back in the market for more money. Even though Uber was operating in only a handful of cities, it was able at this point to show in concrete and credible terms what the future might hold. Typically a fledgling technology business would show investors pie-in-the-sky projections, out-of-thin-air guesses at exponential growth. Uber, however, could extrapolate from its actual growth rates in its first few markets to forecast performance based on the number of cities it was targeting. "The company had nine thousand customers and $1.8 million in net revenue," says Shervin Pishevar, who had recently joined the firm Menlo Ventures and badly wanted to invest in Uber. "So it was tiny. But the metrics were just astounding. My estimate was that it would get to $100 million gross revenue within a year. It did that within six months."

Pishevar was one of several investors who wanted a piece of Uber. Among the most prominent was Andreessen Horowitz, then a two-year-old firm helmed by Marc Andreessen, a cofounder of Netscape. Andreessen Horowitz was media savvy and aggressively self-promotional. It also found early success with an unusual deal. It had been part of an investment group that bought the Internet calling service Skype from eBay—a private-equity transaction rather than a VC play—and quickly flipped the company to Microsoft for a gain of $5 billion for the group. Andreessen's marquee name appealed to Kalanick. Having the backing of such investors conferred legitimacy on start-ups, particularly attractive to an entrepreneur who had toiled in obscurity for as long as Kalanick had.

Uber reached a handshake agreement with Andreessen Horowitz, and Kalanick told a host of investors, including Pishevar, they were out. Disappointed, Pishevar, a bro-hugging bear of a man who routinely mixes business with pleasure, told Kalanick he'd still be interested if things didn't work out with Andreessen Horowitz. Things didn't work out. Andreessen Horowitz had agreed to invest in Uber at a valuation of nearly $375 million, but then got cold feet. Andreessen asked Kalanick to dinner and said he'd like the valuation to be closer to half what they had agreed on. "They just felt it was too pricey," says Kalanick. "I said, 'Look, if I had doubled the revenues, would you do this deal?' And he's like, 'Hell, yes.' And I said, 'Marc, I've got that in three months.' But it was too pricey for them."

Though new to the venture-capital world, Pishevar was already a veteran networker. His family had left Iran during the revolution that brought Ayatollah Khomeini to power, and Pishevar had sold several technology companies by his mid-thirties. He was attending an entrepreneurship conference in Tunisia in October 2011 when Kalanick called to ask if he'd still like to invest. He also asked Pishevar to fly immediately to Dublin, where Kalanick was attending an Internet conference. "We were walking on those ancient cobblestoned streets in Dublin that are really bad for Uber cars, and he starts explaining the full vision that he wasn't really talking about to everyone at the time, which was that he wanted to basically replace car ownership," Pishevar recalls. Menlo Ventures invested $26.5 million at a valuation of $290 million, and Pishevar accepted the relatively demeaning role of observer to the board of directors. Normally an investment of that size and at that stage would have qualified for a full seat on the board.

Pishevar would end up bringing to Uber far more than his firm's money. (He'd also leave Menlo Ventures less than two years later to found his own venture-capital outfit.) While running a video-game-related company several years earlier, Pishevar had developed a personal network of actors and power brokers in Hollywood. Once involved with Uber, he recruited a bevy of these celebrities to invest. The boldface names he lined up included actors Edward Norton, Sophia Bush, Olivia Munn, and Ashton Kutcher. Pishevar also was responsible for bringing in the likes of agent Ari Emanuel, director Lawrence Bender, and music impresario Jay Z. He introduced Kalanick to Amazon CEO Jeff Bezos, whose private investment arm, Bezos Expeditions, took a piece of the action. Another critical new investor was Goldman Sachs, which would go on to act as Uber's unofficial financial adviser as well as a source of much of its nonengineering talent for the next several years.

As Uber grew in popularity, it began to court controversy wherever it went. Washington, D.C., for example, was Uber's sixth U.S. city and the first where it encountered significant official blowback. It launched in November 2011 and the company hired

Rachel Holt, a twenty-eight-year-old former management consultant, as general manager for the city. Holt visited San Francisco in January to attend "Uber Camp," the new-employee
training program that later would be called "Uberversity." Upon
her return to D.C., Washington's taxi commissioner had posted
a message on Twitter stating that Uber was operating an illegal
taxi service. Holt was surprised but not unprepared. Just as Kalanick had concluded in late 2010 that taxi laws didn't apply to
Uber—which didn't own cars and wasn't arranging taxi rides—
Holt thought she was on solid legal ground. "He wasn't citing any
rules," she says. "He was just saying this is illegal."

Then, on the Friday before the Martin Luther King holiday
weekend—Friday the 13th, as it happened—the same taxi commissioner requested a ride on Uber. The service was small enough
that staffers knew all its drivers and could monitor all pickup
requests. "We let him take the ride," says Holt. "We weren't doing
anything wrong." The commissioner, it turns out, traveled to the
Mayflower Hotel, where he had called a press conference. He
proceeded to impound the driver's car and issue a $2,000 ticket.
Holt rushed to contact all Uber's drivers, assuring them the company would pay their fines and help get their cars back. The company also mobilized a social-media campaign to drum up
popular support for its service. It was the first time Uber would
come under significant attack from regulatory officials—but not
the last. In fact, Uber found itself facing down regulators and taxi
companies pretty much everywhere it went. Kalanick considered
Uber's small staff and lack of regulatory experience and realized
he'd need help. He found that help in the person of Bradley Tusk,
a New York political consultant in his mid-thirties who had a

career of relevant experience. As a young law school graduate, Tusk had worked in the administration of New York mayor Mike Bloomberg, as communications director for Senator Charles Schumer, and then, improbably, as the deputy governor of Illinois under soon-to-be-disgraced governor Rod Blagojevich. Tusk then took a job at the investment bank Lehman Brothers, where he designed a never-launched financial product to privatize state lotteries. (Lehman cratered before the product had a chance to test the market.) After running Bloomberg's final re-election campaign, Tusk set up his own political consulting firm, and he was advising big corporations like Pepsi, AT&T, and Walmart in May 2011 when he got a call from Kalanick.

Tusk designed what would become Uber's regulatory game plan for every city it entered. "In each city we'd launch, taxi companies would come at us to shut us down, first through the local taxi commission, then through local and state agencies and legislatures," says Tusk. "We'd run the campaign to stop them, which typically comprised lobbying, PR and grassroots." For the next three years, Tusk's team helped Uber battle in U.S. cities, notably New York, Boston, Philadelphia, Washington, D.C., Miami, Denver, Chicago, Los Angeles, and Las Vegas. The work made Tusk a celebrity in regulatory circles, and he later parlayed his prominence into a business advising start-ups in return for equity stakes. This was in an attempt to replicate one piece of extraordinarily good luck. When Kalanick first called Tusk in 2011, Uber couldn't afford to pay the fee, so Kalanick offered Tusk Uber stock instead. That small piece of Uber was worth more than $100 million five years later.

Launching Uber was like waging a multifront war. In Denver,

for example, the Colorado Public Utilities Commission proposed rules to contain Uber in the months after it started operating, in mid-2012. Uber fought back with a social-media-oriented public-relations blitz that worked with riders who liked the service and drivers eager for the cash they suddenly were earning. In a blog post addressed to the "Uber-Faithful," the company warned that proposed rule changes would make Uber's pricing model illegal (which it compared to telling hotels they couldn't charge by the night), ban Uber drivers from downtown Denver ("TAXI protectionism at its finest"), and make it illegal to partner with limousine companies. Uber urged its supporters to contact the state's governor, John Hickenlooper, directly. In 2014, Hickenlooper signed a bill that lightly regulated Uber and its competitors, effectively legalizing the service.

These battles played out almost everywhere Uber—and Lyft, often behind it—went. In early 2014, for example, the news site *BuzzFeed* counted seventeen active regulatory fights in various U.S. cities, counties, and states. These included a protracted battle in New York City, where one of the bones of contention was the city's demand that Uber share trip data with officials, and Orlando, where proposed rules attempted to force Uber and similar companies to charge 25 percent more than taxis. In most instances a massive lobbying and public-relations onslaught succeeded in allowing the ridesharing companies to operate. But not everywhere. In May 2016, Uber and Lyft left Austin, Texas, after refusing to comply with the city's fingerprinting measures. New ridesharing services willing to comply with Austin's rules quickly offered service there.

Uber's customers were often reliable supporters of the

company, especially in its earliest months in a new market. The convenience of summoning a cheap ride—almost always subsidized by Uber—and being freed from spotty taxi service typically felt too good to be true. But as riders became accustomed to Uber, they inevitably complained about it, often as much as they had complained about cabs. The number-one gripe was Uber's pricing policy. The knock on taxis was that they were often scarce, especially at times of high demand, like rush hour and closing time at bars. Uber's solution was straight out of an economics textbook: it would apply a "surge multiplier" when demand outstripped supply. Its version of dynamic pricing, a tactic popular with airlines and hotels, would have two effects. First, it would encourage more drivers to go to work as they'd have the opportunity to make more money. In economics lingo, the temporary incentive would stimulate supply. Second, higher prices would cause some customers to choose another transportation option, thus reducing demand and lowering wait times for those who were willing to pay more.

In theory, surge pricing worked great. In practice, it infuriated customers and would become a lasting public-relations headache for Uber. The outrage first hit on New Year's Eve in New York in 2011, when some fares were eight times the normal load. In later years, prices would spike on the East Coast during Hurricane Sandy, during blizzards, and in the middle of a hostage crisis in Sydney, Australia. Kalanick exacerbated matters by taking a "get-over-it" attitude with riders. "Someone who is driving a car on a regular occurrence deals with dynamic pricing all the time: it's called gas prices," he told *The New York Times*, shortly after the New Year's incident when some customers paid more than $100 for relatively short rides. Bill Gurley, a prolific blogger and the venture-capital industry's leading public intellectual, a couple years later wrote a 2,500-word treatise defending surge pricing. "The bottom line is that the only real alternative to dynamic pricing is a ton of customers staring at screens that read 'No Cars Available,'" he wrote. "This is the fact that is least appreciated by Uber's critics." He reminded readers of a worse recent outrage than Uber's price hikes, UPS's failure one Christmas to deliver packages because its delivery network was overstretched. Gurley concluded: "Uber has no intention of abandoning dynamic pricing precisely because it is in the consumer's best interest, especially when one understands the true alternatives."

Surge pricing would remain controversial as well as a source of academic fascination for years. In 2015, a group of scholars commissioned by the U.S. Federal Trade Commission published a long analysis of Uber's pricing mechanism, concluding that the company's "black box" algorithm raised "important questions of fairness and transparency."

The acrimony over a topic that was simultaneously wonky and relatable to any passenger also helped introduce the public to a new global commercial character: Travis Kalanick, the "asshole." Suddenly a public figure with his face on the cover of magazines and a highly sought-after speaker on the conference circuit, Kalanick began to be known not only as the scrappy entrepreneur of his self-image but also as a cutthroat businessman with a tin ear to consumer sentiment. In a growing segment of the public's mind, Kalanick was someone for whom economic theory trumped compassion.

Still, Uber was growing rapidly, and surely the criticism was a reflection that people cared about Kalanick's product enough to complain about it. What's more, if he was beginning to feel the heat from the public, he also was gaining fans among like-minded entrepreneurs. Bill Gurley recounts a dinner with Jeff Bezos, an Uber investor, where Bezos praised Kalanick for his entrepreneurial chops. It was the very controversy around Kalanick that had won him praise from Bezos. "He is so correct on surge pricing," Bezos told Gurley. "He is fundamentally, absolutely correct. And a large contingent of the press and others want to talk him out of it. And he stays behind it."

Over the course of 2012 Uber would spread throughout the United States as well as multiple non-U.S. locations, ending the year in twenty-seven markets. As well, it would begin experimenting with product extensions that would change the face of the company. The most important was UberX, which began in July as a service that provided rides in hybrid cars. It was a small-scale response to a new competitor, a company called Lyft, which beginning in May 2012 started a service that enabled anyone with a car to slap a giant pink mustache on the grill and "share" rides with others. Up to this point, Uber had defined itself as an upscale service, with its network of independent contractors consisting of licensed, professional limousine drivers. Now, though it initially stayed away from Lyft's anything-goes approach, it was ready to move down-market. "The best way to describe it is that the experience will be efficient, but not as elegant," Kalanick told the tech news site *AllThingsD*. "You won't see an UberX driver opening the door for you."

Kalanick also began to describe Uber publicly as a "platform" capable of moving around more than people. "Uber is the cross of lifestyle and logistics," he told *AllThingsD*. To illustrate the possibilities, Uber began a series of marketing stunts, like delivering hot barbecue at a conference in Austin, ice cream in the heat of summer, and roses on Valentine's Day. The stunts were just that: gimmicks to demonstrate what Uber was capable of. And for the foreseeable future essentially all the company's revenues came from taking a commission from the trips in which drivers delivered passengers to their destinations. The contours of a tech-driven platform approach began to show promise. Delivering food proved relatively similar to ferrying people. Marketing stunts like these presaged spinoff businesses like UberEats, a food delivery service. Slowly but surely, Uber proved that it could extend its reach into industries other than transportation. Expansion remained theoretical, but Uber had the ways and means to make it a reality.

CHAPTER 7
Growing Pains

I n the spring of 2012, San Franciscans started to see a strange sight on their city's streets. Already, thanks to Uber, it had become commonplace for slick luxury sedans to pull up in front of a home whose inhabitants had no business traveling in such grandeur. (Personal story: Shortly after Uber's debut, three recent college graduates—loud, unruly, disrespectful, hard-partying recent college graduates—moved into the apartment above my family. It was initially a total head scratcher to watch the three young men saunter out of the building at 11:00 P.M., dressed as if for a frat party, and hop into a waiting Town Car. They apparently knew about Uber before I did.) The new, jarring experience swung to the other extreme. Run-of-the-mill passenger cars driven by ordinary people popped up around town with a giant pink mustache plastered on the front.

The young company associated with the pink grill ornament was Lyft, the first of a new breed of so-called ridesharing companies. (Others included Sidecar in the United States and Hailo in the United Kingdom.) "Ridesharing" was a new and nuanced term of art among tech companies. Only professional drivers sat behind the wheels of taxis—and, at the time, limos operating on the Uber platform. Lyft was different. In fact, it positioned itself as the antithesis of its better-known competitor. If Uber was "Everyone's Private Driver," charging a hefty premium over cabs, Lyft represented a friendly neighbor who'd invite you into her front seat, fist-bump you once you sat down, and charge you merely the cost of the "shared" ride plus a "donation" for her trouble. What's more, that price might well be less than a cab ride.

Sharing was a misnomer, given that Lyft's drivers were out to make a buck every bit as much as Uber's. But by promoting the fiction of a friendly gesture rather than a transaction, Lyft could make an argument, however thin, that its trips weren't commercial. If so, Lyft reasoned they weren't illegal taxi rides and didn't fall under any regulator's jurisdiction. In reality, Uber worked only with licensed livery drivers; Lyft's drivers were freelancing amateurs. Yet Lyft had one critical similarity with Uber in that its smartphone app adopted the push-a-button/get-a-ride simplicity that catapulted Uber into the limelight.

The two companies were a study in contrasts, especially in their origins. Uber grew out of the San Francisco "brogrammer" culture and Garrett Camp's delight in rolling in style. Lyft sprang from the idealistic mind of Logan Green, who'd served on the Santa Barbara, California, public transit board when he was a university student in that seaside town. Green's passion was to encourage alternatives to driving. On a postcollege trip to Zimbabwe, he took note of the efficient if informal system of ride-sharing the locals used. He went back to the United States and started a carpooling software company called Zimride, inspired by his trip to Africa.

In 2007, Green got connected through a mutual friend to John Zimmer, a junior banker at Lehman Brothers who had studied the hotel business at Cornell University. Zimmer and Green started working together, and three months before Lehman's fall, Zimmer quit banking to join Zimride full time. (He claimed no prescience regarding the doomed investment bank and says a colleague told him he was "crazy to leave a sure thing like Lehman for a silly carpool start-up.") Zimmer had taken a course at Cornell on "green cities" and had been captivated ever since by the idea of making cities more efficient. Enchanted by Green's concept of using software to arrange congestion-reducing carpools, Zimmer joined forces with Green, and the two relocated to San Francisco. "We built a profitable business selling carpool systems to universities and companies, kind of replacing the old bulletin board that existed on college campuses," says Zimmer, who became the company's president. A third product line matched travelers on long-haul routes, like San Francisco to Los Angeles.

Zimride was a modest success, but its founders surveyed the start-up landscape in San Francisco and saw a bigger opportunity. In the parlance of Silicon Valley, they decided to pivot. They would take their knowledge of arranging rides for large groups of loosely affiliated people and apply it to the business model of Uber, a company they saw as catering to the 1 percent. "At that point Uber was just doing black cars and limos," says Zimmer. "That was never that interesting to us. We thought: 'What if we could do this for personal vehicles?'"

After writing the software for a smartphone app over three weeks in the spring of 2012, Zimride launched a new service in San Francisco called Lyft. It was a hit, especially with young people who shunned the elitist stigma of riding in a limousine. Says Zimmer: "It was so popular so quickly we had to create a wait list." Uber's customers hadn't needed to be told how to be chauffeured, but Lyft's unique approach required some consumer training. "One thing that we had to solve that they didn't in doing the limo experience was that this was a very strange behavioral change," says Zimmer. "If I told you then that we were going to get people to ride in other people's cars, you would have said I was crazy. It's what your parents told you never to do. It's also not aspirational to get in the backseat of someone's Honda Accord." So Lyft encouraged riders to hop in front, which is where you'd sit with a friend. "Sitting in the backseat was something you do in a black car," says Zimmer. And the pink mustache? That, he says, was simply a way to make people smile. (The mustache was also a smart marketing move: passersby tended to want to know why a fluffy pink mustache was attached to the front of cars on the streets of San Francisco.)

Uber caught wind of Lyft, but initially it decided "ridesharing" not only wasn't its thing but likely represented a violation of rules regulating taxis. "We watched it closely," says Ryan Graves, Uber's head of operations. "And we were keenly in touch with the reality that it was against the rules." At first, Lyft assumed Uber would leave the grubby end of the market to them. "They had this view of a luxury lifestyle brand, and they had always been thinking about what else can they give to people instantly," says Zimmer, referring to Uber's experiments with delivering ice cream, kittens, and the like. "We thought that was a very entitled way of looking at it, like 'I want things to come to me. And nice things.'" Uber moving to personal vehicles, says Zimmer, "was not necessarily in their DNA. But as they saw what a massive business opportunity it was, it was impossible to ignore it."

In fact, Uber initially tiptoed into the new market. In mid-2012 it experimented with offering inexpensive rides in fuel-efficient hybrid cars, calling the new service UberX. Yet as Lyft grew, especially in Uber's home market, Uber was clearly rattled. Kalanick publicly showed his ire. On a March morning in 2013 he posted a message on Twitter suggesting that Uber had spoken to "dozens" of Lyft drivers who hadn't seen Lyft's insurance policy. About twenty minutes later, Zimmer replied, "Travis—seems like you're fishing for info and might need some insurance." For two hours the two continued their public spat, with Kalanick accusing Zimmer of dodging his question, Zimmer asking why Uber didn't conduct criminal background checks, and Kalanick suggesting that Zimmer visit Uber's headquarters for a chat. Tiring of the debate, Zimmer suggested that seeing as Kalanick wanted the last word, "I'll let you have it so I can get to work." He added the phrase "#respect"—which in Twitterspeak meant that Kalanick ought to have shown Zimmer some. Unable to resist, Kalanick shot back, "you've got a lot of catching up to do . . . #clone." These were fighting words. Over time, Uber would frequently use "clone" to denigrate Lyft, including in its presentations for investors. It apparently stung that the smaller and less well-funded company had beaten Uber to the punch in the market that only later would account for its stratospheric growth.

It was a mistake Uber decided to correct—and never make again. Kalanick wrote a white paper in April 2013 justifying Uber's entry into the market for cars driven by amateur drivers. He concluded that the absence of regulatory action against Lyft in San Francisco amounted to a tacit approval to operate. As well, letting another company test the market was a painful lesson for Uber. "We realized we can't let a competitor get ahead of us in any market that we're in," says Graves. "We learned a lot about the need for speed and being first to market." In mid-2013 Uber executed a pivot of its own, repositioning UberX and beginning to recruit drivers for its new service. It made no effort to simulate Lyft's goofy hood ornament or faux-friendly demeanor; Uber was about getting an inexpensive ride from point A to point B as quickly as possible.

The battle heated up rapidly. Lyft and Uber had begun to square off against each other across the United States. Lyft, in six U.S. cities a year after starting to offer ridesharing, sold its Zimride business to the car-rental company Enterprise Holdings, which continues to operate it and still caters to universities and companies. (Lyft, Zimride's ridesharing product before the sale, became the company's name.) Uber went through a product repositioning as well. UberX, initially promoted as an "eco-friendly" alternative to requesting a limo, became Uber's taxi-beating

A young Travis Kalanick.

Kalanick's fourth-grade football team; he's number 21.

The Scour team on the last day of its existence. From left to right, Kevin Smilak, Craig Grossman, Travis Kalanick, Dan Rodrigues, and Michael Todd.

The Red Swoosh team in 2002: Travis Kalanick (second from left), Francesco Fabbrocino (standing, fourth from left), Evan Tsang (third from right), Rob Bowman (far right).

Garrett Camp (left) and Travis Kalanick in front of the
Eiffel Tower during their pivotal 2008 trip.

The Uber team in the beginning. From left to right: Curtis Chambers, Travis Kalanick, Stefan
Schmeisser, Conrad Whelan, Jordan Bonnet, Austin Geidt, Ryan Graves, Ryan McKillen.

The early UberCab Web site.

Edward Norton was Rider One in Los Angeles in 2012.

Ryan Graves and Austin Geidt jamming in Uber's early days.

Shervin Pishevar and Travis Kalanick, moments after signing the term sheet for Series B funding in Dublin, October 2011.

Kalanick with two employees at Uberversity Happy Hour, an event for new hires, June 2013.

The Uber team parties in Miami, October 2013: Ryan Graves (left), Austin Geidt (second from left), and Shervin Pishevar (far right).

At the 2014 Recode Conference, Kalanick says Uber is battling "an asshole named Taxi."

Kalanick with the engineering team at the 2015 Uber Hackathon at the San Francisco headquarters.

Kalanick with Bernard Lo, anchor of CNBC Asia, at the 2016 World Economic Forum in Tianjin, China.

A prototype of Uber's self-driving car displayed at the Uber Advanced Technologies Center in Pittsburgh, 2016.

offering. What had been Uber was now UberBlack, which in time became a tiny percentage of Uber's business. Lyft may have had a new approach, but due to its head start with limos, Uber had a broader network in which to insert UberX. It operated in seventy-seven markets worldwide by the end of 2013.

Size didn't prevent Uber from feeling threatened by its pesky and preternaturally cheerful competitor. To keep Lyft in its place, Uber repeatedly used aggressive tactics against it. In 2014, the technology news site *The Verge* published a stunning exposé of Uber's dirty-pool behavior in New York, where it hired temporary workers to use "burner" phones to request Lyft rides only to recruit drivers to its side. (The anonymous phones were to throw Lyft off the scent of who was punking them.) In e-mails, Uber encouraged its recruiters to "#shavethestache." Uber owned up to "Operation SLOG," saying its recruitment drive was fair competition. But after allowing Lyft to build one new market under its nose, Uber was ever vigilant about not letting it happen again. Both companies maintained a constant dialogue with their drivers, aiming to refine their offerings as well as to glean competitive intelligence. When Uber caught wind around the same time that Lyft was about to launch a carpooling service, Lyft Line, Uber announced UberPool, its own carpool product, the night before.

Lyft would prove a stubborn number two. It raised first tens of millions, then hundreds of millions of dollars. Its most prominent early backer was Andreessen Horowitz, the same firm that had snubbed Uber in 2011. Lyft would continue to feel stymied by Uber, and not just in the competition for riders. "For a

company so confident that it's a single-horse race, they've histor-
ically been quite scared of us," says Zimmer. As Lyft has discussed
stakes with investors, he says, Uber has "tried to talk to whoever
we're talking to, somehow knowing sometimes pretty close to
when we're talking to them and sometimes offering discounts,
as long as they agree not to invest in us." As time wore on, the
two companies began to look more and more alike, with many
drivers registering to offer rides through both services, depending
on which company's short-term incentives were better. Lyft would
never come close to Uber in size. But its mere existence forced
Uber to spend far more money than it had anticipated, denting and
sometimes extinguishing its profitability. The cheerful pink mustache most certainly did not bring a smile to Uber's corporate face.

◉───◉

Uber had entered its start-up-company adolescent phase, a phenomenon but nowhere near the titan it aspired to be. To get there,
it would need to build itself into a modern corporation, a process
that proceeded in fits and starts. Internally, the company was
defined by a grueling pace and a can-do attitude, a state of mind
insiders called the "Uber hustle." So much about its business
was new that experimentation was the norm. Uber found itself
cobbling together solutions to problems no other company had
ever confronted. The times called for a special kind of employee
too, one who worked long hours, made the rules rather than followed them, and more often than not was young and unattached.
Uber workers viewed the intermingling of work with their personal life as a benefit, not a negative. It wasn't uncommon for early

employees to move around the company working in areas as varied as customer support, brand management, or product development.

It was a frenetic time of trial and error. Tactics would work for a while, only to fizzle out, particularly in driver recruitment and consumer marketing. For example, in any new city the company would expend tremendous effort and cash recruiting customers. Offering $20 for a first ride was a tactic that worked, but only to a point. Steering discounted rides to wedding planners was popular for a bit too, until too many wedding-goers had already tried Uber. The company went through the same drill to recruit drivers. Advertising on Craigslist was effective for a time. Then Uber would focus on recruiting taxi drivers. When that supply was tapped out, Uber turned its attention to schoolteachers, attractive for their flexible schedules and desire for extra cash.

Uber was also surfing, and innovating on top of, an increasingly powerful industry wave, the rise of smartphones. An internal presentation described Uber as "mobile first," a popular expression at the time, but with the word "first" crossed out and replaced with "only." The technology changed so quickly that Uber could dramatically improve its offering as new features became available. Early iPhones, for example, allowed for only spotty tracking of drivers by riders. Later versions let Uber make the little black cars zip along on the app's map far more fluidly.

As it expanded, Uber centralized certain critical functions, like software development, while pushing out day-to-day business decisions to its teams in the field. A city typically launched with just three people: a general manager; an operations manager for "community," the company's word for its pool of riders; and an operations manager for "partners," its preferred term for drivers. (Because Uber takes commission from drivers, the company also calls drivers "customers," a confusing term that would annoy independent contractors; only passengers pay Uber, which takes its cut and then pays drivers.)

Prospective top managers were subjected to intense grilling by Kalanick as part of an interview process that would have fit in at a management consulting firm. He asked each candidate for a city general manager job to prepare a "city presentation," a PowerPoint deck that showed how the potential executive would build out a market for Uber. Pierre-Dimitri Gore-Coty, a Frenchman who had been working for a hedge fund in London, prepared such a presentation in the fall of 2012, hoping to become general manager for Paris. A short while later he found himself on Skype with Kalanick and Graves. Kalanick's goal in interviewing candidates is to try "to simulate real-life interaction in an office," says Gore-Coty. "Travis spent ten to fifteen minutes discussing my previous experiences, asking me about my investments and my analysis of the media industry"—topics that might have little bearing on Uber. Kalanick told Gore-Coty they were engaging in a "jam," an expression that was lost on the Frenchman at the time. "I'd never heard that word before."

Kalanick and Graves, as CEO and head of operations, respectively, were the dominant players in Uber's early executive suite. Garrett Camp never joined the company as an employee or took a salary. Instead, he remained CEO of StumbleUpon, which he had bought back from eBay in 2009. He was, however, Uber's chairman and a frequent presence at the company. Camp became a billionaire as Uber's valuation skyrocketed, and he was also one of the very few Uber shareholders to sell a significant number of shares on the private market, well before the company's initial public offering. But from its earliest days he sidestepped the burden of running what became a complicated company. Camp left StumbleUpon in 2012, and rather than become an executive at Uber, the following year he started an investment firm called Expa. "Even though I still talk about Uber with people a lot and have a lot of inbound"—meaning various people in Uber's orbit bring information to him—"and even though it's still on my mind like every day a little bit, it really is an advisory role at this point," he'd reflect years later. "It's Travis's thing now, not mine."

Kalanick began to build out his management team, often recruiting talent from some of the technology industry's biggest players. Uber's valuation kept rising, which provided Kalanick with a currency—Uber equity—that allowed him to poach talent from around the Valley. He especially coveted executives who had helped the industry's biggest players make the transition from start-ups to giants. Facebook, for instance, had a function called "growth," a team of people who assisted product and other teams in hitting their goals to move the business forward. In mid-2013 Kalanick hired Ed Baker from Facebook as head of growth. Baker, who had founded a dating Web site while at Harvard University, was an expert in "virality," the part art/part scientific technique of making an Internet product grow exponentially. The key to helping an organization grow, he says, is zeroing in on the appropriate target. At Facebook, initially this was monthly active users. At Uber, "we started by trying to determine our goal." His team of five that Kalanick assigned him from various parts of the company homed in on its target: weekly trips. "Having that one core metric helped. Everyone at Facebook understood monthly average users was the goal. At Uber, we knew we needed more riders and drivers and to reduce churn of existing ones."

Baker's group was free to try to tweak any aspect of Uber's techniques to achieve its growth goals, whether in marketing, finance, product development, or other areas. Kalanick monitored the group's progress closely. "We used to meet with Travis every Friday morning," says Baker. "We'd start preparing for those meetings at seven P.M. on Thursday night and be at the office until three A.M. At every meeting he'd have a 'today' card where he'd want something done that day. It was his way of removing the white space" between planning and execution. As an example, Baker says his group wanted to test a sign-up button for drivers on Uber's Web site, a move the brand design team opposed because they thought it was ugly. Kalanick's "today" order trumped the brand group's concerns. "The button quickly became the single largest source of organic sign-ups for us," says Baker, organic meaning free, or not generated by paid marketing. "So it was a very good 'today' decision."

In early 2014, Kalanick hired a former Amazon executive named Jeff Holden to oversee Uber's products. Holden had worked with Jeff Bezos during his pre-Amazon career on Wall Street at a firm called D. E. Shaw and then at Amazon. When he connected with Kalanick he was at Groupon, an e-commerce site in Chicago that had grown at a torrid pace and then stalled.

His assignment was to professionalize Uber's product development. "When I got here very little new product development was going on," says Holden. "We were mostly fixing bugs, the things that you could do but not the things that you should do. It was just a mess." Holden had seen it before. "When small start-ups get to a certain scale they hit gridlock because the way you do everything as a small company is to just kind of get in a room and talk about it. There's no need to have a significant organization."

Holden added process and structure. He also highlighted two critical aspects of Uber's product he found lacking: a rider's ability to communicate beforehand where he or she wanted to go and a driver's ability to navigate there. "I remember getting picked up in an UberX, and I would tell the person where I'm going and they'd pull over and they'd type into this little TomTom device or whatever, and I'm like, 'Oh, this is so bad.'" He mandated new "no-brainer" features that changed the Uber experience: destination, inputted by the rider; and turn-by-turn navigation on the Uber driver app.

Uber went live with both features in August 2014 and in one fell swoop drastically lowered the turnaround time for rides. It also foreshadowed a future battle. Before Uber, the difference between a good cab driver and a bad one was their knowledge of their city's streets. (The test for a London cabbie is called exactly that: "The Knowledge.") GPS-guided mapping told a driver where to go, rendering personal knowledge obsolete. The driver's value was reduced to turning the steering wheel and working the accelerator and brakes. When would driving the car, like knowing where to go, be outsourced to a computer too? Holden was asking the question too, and soon enough he would address it.

◉────────────────────────────────◉

David Krane was on the verge of completing the most important deal of his life when Travis Kalanick called him and began the conversation by saying, "Hear me out." These were not the words he wanted to hear. Krane's career had followed an unusual trajectory. An early public-relations executive at Google, he had shifted to the role of investor for Google's in-house venture arm. What he lacked in investing experience, he made up for with his vast knowledge of Google and its idiosyncratic ways. An investment from Google Ventures could be a pathway to strategic relationships with Google. This is precisely what he and Kalanick had been discussing in the summer of 2013 as a reason for Google to take a stake in Uber.

His was among several firms vying to invest in Uber. The "bakeoff" among them had gone well for Krane. Kalanick had led him to believe Google Ventures was one of two finalists to write a single check for $250 million, valuing Uber at $3.5 billion. Then came Kalanick's hear-me-out call, a signal that there was a glitch. It turns out Kalanick had spent the previous months being romanced by a different kind of investor, a private-equity firm called TPG, or Texas Pacific Group. A TPG partner named David Trujillo had spearheaded an effort to get the firm involved in earlier-stage Internet investments, in contrast to the more usual controlling stakes in mature companies that PE shops focus on. Trujillo had befriended Kalanick, meeting him for beers in San Francisco after the former put his kids to bed and as the latter was leaving the office. The two would go deep on Uber's business, with Kalanick frequently opening his laptop to call up data including driver cohorts, retention rates, lifetime value of drivers and riders, rider acquisition costs, and so on. TPG had been doing its own research too. It sent its pre-MBA analysts out on multiple Uber rides in New York and San Francisco with a set list of questions for drivers. It was surprised by how much drivers valued the flexibility that came with choosing their own hours and the safety afforded them by cashless transactions.

Before now, Kalanick had been in the position of wooing investors. Now the roles were reversed. TPG in particular was pursuing Uber. David Bonderman, one of the firm's two founders, had joined the board of General Motors in 2009 as part of the government-sponsored bankruptcy process. He arranged for GM vice chairman Stephen Girsky to visit San Francisco to become acquainted with the company that one day might have a giant impact on car ownership. (Girsky hadn't heard of Uber before Bonderman mentioned it to him.) In the summer of 2013, Bonderman and Trujillo invited Kalanick to accompany them on a tour of Asia on TPG's private jet so he could meet business and government leaders. TPG, which had invested in many regulated companies over the years, told Kalanick how helpful it could be with regulators.

In August 2013, Kalanick had decided he wanted TPG as an investor. Given that Google Ventures had expected to be the sole investor, he hit on a novel way to include TPG. He knew Garrett Camp was willing to sell a portion of his Uber holdings, partly to fund a new investment company called Expa. (Normally, Kalanick was vehemently opposed to Uber's employees and investors selling shares of Uber, though he eventually allowed some employees to sell a portion of their shares to the company; for Camp, without whom Uber wouldn't have existed, he made an early exception.) Instead of TPG investing directly in Uber, it would buy around $100 million in stock from Camp in an obscure maneuver called a Waverly loan that would leave Camp and TPG with obligations to each other. "I knew I was selling at a loss," says Camp, who saw the maneuver as a plus in order to bring in TPG. At Kalanick's insistence, Bonderman, not Trujillo, would join the board. He made a similar request of Google Ventures, asking Krane to be merely a board observer. At the same time, he invited David Drummond, Google's longtime policy chief, to join the board. As with his preference for Bill Gurley over Matt Cohler at Benchmark, Kalanick put a premium on experience, status, and name recognition.

Ever the phrasemaker, Kalanick softened the blow for Krane having to share an investment he thought would be his alone by telling him that TPG scratched a different itch than Google Ventures. "You guys are the digital, and they are the analog," he told Krane. In a blog post announcing the $258 million investment—while not mentioning that TPG's "investment" went to Camp, not Uber—Kalanick first used the phrase "bits and atoms" to refer to Google's and TPG's respective strengths. This digital knowhow combined with real-world experience was meant to describe Uber's newest investors. Kalanick also meant it as a description of Uber itself.

⊙————————————————————————⊙

Shortly after the Google-TPG investment, Kalanick made another key hire, Emil Michael, who would be head of "business" at Uber. Trained as a lawyer, Michael had worked for a couple minor Valley players, Tellme Networks and Klout. He had flirted with top jobs at streaming-music company Spotify and fitness tracker Jawbone, and was still casting about for the right position. As a prestigious White House Fellow in between tech-company stints, he had also been a special assistant to U.S. secretary of defense Robert Gates, working on "crazy-ass cybersecurity stuff," among other things. "I spent a lot of time in Afghanistan, Iraq, and Pakistan, figuring how to use tech to help the troops do mobile payments," he says. "We would pay some of the Afghans to defend their own country. But then their warlords would steal their money. So we did mobile payments so that they couldn't steal the cash."

Michael brought his battle skills to Uber, initially to craft partnerships with companies like American Express and United Airlines that could integrate Uber's service into their mobile apps. Having been involved in fund-raising in past ventures, Michael told Kalanick he'd be willing to do the same at Uber. "Travis said, 'Emil, we just raised $250 million. I don't think we'll ever need to raise money again."

Circumstances suggested otherwise. With Uber combating Lyft at home and multiple players around the world, the company's capital needs suddenly seemed endless. By mid-2014 Kalanick had indeed tapped Michael to oversee fund-raising. But Kalanick wanted things done his way. "Travis taught me something on fund-raising that I hadn't learned in my whole career," says Michael. "He said not to get attached to the outcome, but instead to get attached to the process." In effect, he wanted Michael to run a well-organized auction, offering investors the opportunity to name their "price," meaning the valuation of the company, and the amount they wanted to invest. "I was religious about this process. I kept everyone on the right time lines. I said the same thing to everyone, so I never gave anyone any special treatment."

In June 2014, less than nine months after Uber had raised $258 million at a valuation of $3.5 billion, Uber raised another $1.2 billion from mutual-fund investors Wellington Management, Fidelity Investments, and BlackRock, among others, valuing Uber at $17 billion. The funding round was notable for two reasons. First, the investors were not from venture capital or private equity, signaling that Uber had broadened its financial appeal to the most mainstream, non-tech-focused investors. Second, because of its process-oriented approach, it ended up being valued far more highly than it expected. Says Michael: "We thought this was going to be an $8 billion valuation."

Flush with cash and surrounded by the buzz of hypergrowth, Uber would end 2014 as a global phenomenon, operating in 262 markets around the world. It was also the year the company's reputation shifted from disruptive darling to brash bully, a sneering brawler waging a multifront war against all comers. Taxi companies, regulators, politicians, competitors, journalists, its own drivers, even women: all could justifiably feel aggrieved by something Uber said or did. Its offender-in-chief was its public face and chief executive, Travis Kalanick, who prided himself on speaking his mind. He seemed incapable, in public or in private, of holding back, as if his outspokenness were a DNA-imprinted aspect of who he was, like the pigment in his eyes or the pitch of his voice. His widely quoted whoppers sometimes had an intellectually defensible ring to them. Yet they suggested a shocking lack of empathy or, at the very least, an inability to know when to keep quiet.

Kalanick had a particular problem with how he spoke about women. It didn't help that Silicon Valley's was a male-dominated "bro" culture, the alpha males being computer programmers and venture capitalists, two fields where women were scarce. The most feminist of men in the Valley would come to understand that unconscious bias was rife in the tech community. But Kalanick had little patience for such nuance. Many of Uber's top executives were women: its head of North American operations, its expansion chief, its general counsel, to name a few. An equal-opportunity manager, perhaps, Kalanick couldn't escape his alpha-male reputation. With a patois that reflected the hip-hop lyrics of his San Fernando Valley youth, he spoke approvingly of being a "baller" (Urban Dictionary: "a thug that has made it to the big time") and once compared his role arranging rides to being a "frickin' pimp." (He was referring to cars, not women. But the word choice was telling.) He had a habit of comparing his company, whether Red Swoosh or Uber, to a spouse, sometimes an abusive one. The metaphor made a weird kind of sense from the perspective of a passionate entrepreneur but sounded odd out of context. In early 2014, he acknowledged to a *GQ* writer, one bent on capturing the testosterone-tinged aura of the go-go Uber experience, that his newfound success improved his desirability with the ladies. Kalanick joked that he could now land women as easily as Uber could summon cars. "Yeah, we call that Boob-er," *GQ* quoted him saying.

Uber would never be able to shake the accusation of endemic misogyny. Since Uber began its rapid expansion into cities all over the world, it has been dogged by reports that women have been propositioned, threatened, and even assaulted by drivers. For example, in 2016, a journalist at the Boston.com Web site named Allison Pohle wrote a harrowing account of an Uber ride she took. She got into a car after matching its license plate with the car designated in her app, as Uber advises passengers to do. The car had only two doors, in violation of Uber's policies, and it was more convenient for her to sit in the front seat. The driver locked the doors and propositioned Pohle, which she described in detail in the article. Pohle was able to get out of the car physically unharmed—but terrified. Furthermore, when she reached out to Uber, a customer-service representative apologized and gave her a $30 credit—but initially failed to confirm that the driver had been punished or kicked off the platform.

The sentiment also reached into the workforce of Uber itself. In February 2017, a former Uber engineer named Susan Fowler posted a story online titled "Reflecting on One Very, Very Strange Year at Uber." She described allegations of having been sexually harassed by her male superior and then having her complaints ignored by Uber's human resources department. Kalanick took to Twitter to call the allegations "abhorrent and against everything Uber stands for and believes in." He also said the post was the first he'd heard of Fowler's complaint, and he formed a committee that included board member Arianna Huffington and former U.S. attorney general Eric Holder to investigate.

None of this improved Uber's reputation among women, who already were questioning the company's record. True, Uber offered advantages over taxis in that the ride could be tracked, the identity of the driver recorded. As well, the human condition is what it is: Uber drivers are hardly the only people to behave badly toward women. And yet the very newness of the "platform" that Uber enabled exacerbated the problem. Taxi drivers are regulated everywhere, and most cities post a complaint number prominently in the backseat of the cab along with the driver's ID number. Uber repeatedly would appear to be insufficiently responsive to such complaints. Indeed, as a new and private company it frequently was unresponsive to all sorts of gripes, and not just from frightened passengers. But because of its size and prominence, Uber had a tough time shaking the notion that women should shun it. Indeed, the news site *BuzzFeed* published a report that claimed that an analysis of Uber's customer-service complaints showed thousands of mentions of the words "rape" and "sexual assault." The company disputed *BuzzFeed*'s report at length, noting that the word "rate" often was misspelled as "rape" and also that the letters spelling out "rape" appear in names like "Draper." Uber said that in a three-year period it analyzed data, it found 170 instances alleging sexual assault, or 1 in every 3.3 million trips.

The bottom line was that the perception hurt the company's bottom line. Every benefit of the power of Uber's technology could prove creepy in the wrong hands. A bad experience with an aggressive driver is one thing. It's another thing altogether when the driver knows the passenger's name and where she lives. And as the "Boob-er" incident and others have proven, Uber's top executives were digging themselves out of holes when it came to being sensitive to such issues.

Over and over again, Kalanick was insensitive to customers' concerns. Kalanick's unemotional defense of dynamic pricing grated for those who equated the practice with price gouging. Anyone who whined about surge pricing, in his eyes, was too thick to understand the laws of supply and demand. He mercilessly, and publicly, thumbed his nose at public officials who supported taxi companies. At times, his fervor completely missed its target. "We're in a political campaign where the candidate is Uber and the opponent is an asshole named Taxi," he told an interviewer in mid-2014. The quote was widely repeated as Kalanick having called taxi drivers assholes. That he meant to disparage taxi company owners, not working-stiff hacks, was lost in translation. "We have to bring out the truth about how dark and dangerous and evil the taxi side of the industry is," he said, a line that didn't get the same attention as his "asshole" comment.

Kalanick also displayed an insouciant, get-over-it disregard for the plight of Uber drivers, the lifeblood of his company. A year before Uber invested in robotic-vehicle software, and therefore at a time he easily could have sidestepped the subject, he addressed the impact autonomy would have on his business. "The magic of self-driving vehicles is that the reason Uber could be expensive is that you're not just paying for the car, you're paying for the other dude in the car," he said in the same interview, an appearance at the influential tech-industry Code conference in Rancho Palos Verdes, California. "So when there's no other dude in the car, the cost of taking an Uber anywhere becomes cheaper than owning a vehicle." Asked how Uber drivers might view this, he made things worse. "If I were talking to one of the drivers we partner with, I'd say, 'Look, this is the way the world's going to go and if Uber doesn't go there it's not going to exist, so that's just the way of the world.' It's the way of technology and progress."

Kalanick would never dig himself out of the hole he'd dug with drivers. In fact, he'd dig it deeper. In early 2017, a longtime UberBlack driver challenged Kalanick on the effects price cuts were having on drivers. He caught Kalanick losing his temper on video: "Some people don't like to take responsibility for their own shit," Kalanick told the driver, who had complained that he'd lost nearly $100,000 and declared personal bankruptcy. The driver leaked the video to *Bloomberg BusinessWeek*, which published it. Kalanick said he was "ashamed" and promised to seek leadership help and to "grow up."

The unguarded moment was proof to Kalanick's critics that his cold-heartedness amounted to a political statement. After all, his Twitter avatar, a thumbnail image that users choose to describe themselves, was the cover of the Ayn Rand book *The Fountainhead*. Rand, a mid-twentieth-century novelist and polemicist, had promoted a philosophy known as Objectivism, an extreme belief in the power of capitalism and technological progress as well as the pernicious effects of government. She tended to be popular with campus Republicans and other collegians experiencing their first taste of intellectual freedom.

It wasn't that much of a stretch to conclude that Kalanick lived by Rand's up-with-progress/down-with-regulation credo. But he figured out that the label wouldn't help him much with the public at large. In the fall of 2014, *Fortune* magazine named Kalanick, then thirty-eight, to its "40-under-40" list of outstanding young businesspeople. The accompanying article on Kalanick noted his fondness for Rand. Kalanick e-mailed me to complain. "There is this crazy meme on the Internet that I am some kind of Ayn Rand disciple," he wrote. He liked to post images on Twitter from books he'd read, he said. "A few years ago I read *The Fountainhead* and put it up as my avatar, not having any idea the political ramification." Now, he wrote, the "Internet has not let it go," despite his having changed his avatar to Alexander Hamilton after having read the popular biography by Ron Chernow. (Kalanick was not jumping on the *Hamilton* bandwagon; the popular musical opened off-Broadway in February 2015, and on Broadway that August.) "Of course, no one calls me a raging Federalist for having Hamilton up on Twitter . . . [or] a lunatic *Ender's Game* [a science-fiction novel by Orson Scott Card] fanatic when I had that up."

If Kalanick was feeling the heat, it would only get worse for him and for Uber. The "Operation SLOG" campaign against Lyft had solidified a sense of Uber's nefariousness among a growing slice of the tech-aware public. "Hopefully people understand what an evil company UBER is and boycott their service," read one comment on *The Verge*, which published the exposé of Uber's campaign against Lyft. Said another: "What can you expect when UBER's CEO is another one of those Ayn-Rand loving libertarian nutjobs." It became politically correct in some coastal cities to avoid Uber altogether. Then, in November 2014, Uber hosted a dinner in New York with influential journalists in which it hoped to put the company in a better light. The meal was supposed to be off the record, but the editor of *BuzzFeed*, a news site whose name speaks to its mission, quoted Emil Michael as having suggested that Uber might investigate the background of certain journalists who seemed to have a vendetta against Uber.

The ensuing firestorm cemented Uber's reputation as the bad boy of Silicon Valley. Michael apologized to the journalist he had singled out, but the damage was done. The next month, a largely flattering profile of Uber in *The Guardian* in the United Kingdom began: "Pity the put-upon urban dweller with a conscience. If it isn't enough that he or she has to worry about carbon emissions, social inequality, non-taxpaying coffee chains and any number of other ethical concerns, there is now the added guilt of using Uber, the smartphone app for hailing cabs." At an industry awards ceremony in San Francisco a couple months later the comedian T. J. Miller, popular for his portrayal of the perennially stoned company founder Erlich Bachman on the hit HBO show *Silicon Valley*, quipped that Kalanick deserved an award for "constantly stepping in shit."

It was a precarious moment for Uber: even as its business was picking up speed its image was cratering. "They completely lost the narrative," bemoaned Chris Sacca, the early Uber investor and adviser, who by this time had had a falling-out with Kalanick over Sacca's attempt to buy the shares of other investors. (For years, Kalanick personally kept a lid on the pre-IPO selling of Uber shares and sold none himself.) David Plouffe, the Obama campaign chief who had joined the company that fall to oversee communications and policy, called the events of the year a series of "unforced errors." And Ryan Graves wistfully referred to the period as "our tough time." Reaching for a silver lining, he equated the spate of horrible publicity to what a listed company experiences when its stock craters. "That was a time when our ticker was low and it was rough," he reflects two years later. "But generally I think we're better off for it. Those kinds of experiences are actually good for an organization and good for individuals who can come out of it on top." It wasn't, of course, Uber's last "tough time."

CHAPTER 8

Juggernaut

By the beginning of 2015 Uber confronted more than a perception problem. Despite its size, it was still more of a scrappy start-up than a sophisticated operation. Yet its charm was wearing thin as its pugnacious and seat-of-the-pants ways bordered on reckless and irresponsible. In other words, while the automobiles that carried its customers may have moved down-market from luxury sedans to common passenger cars, Uber itself needed a considerable upgrade. The company required everything from top talent with experience running global enterprises to the business processes more associated with the giant corporation it was becoming rather than the Silicon Valley upstart it had been.

Its failings were particularly apparent in its approach to safety, in terms of the protection of both the information entrusted to it and the people in its cars. In short, Uber's data, drivers, and riders weren't as secure as they needed to be. Uber's data was voluminous and uniquely powerful. To make its service work, the company had collected license and insurance information for each driver as well as credit card numbers and mobile-phone numbers for every rider. The very information that enabled Uber's magical service—press a button and a car appears for a cashless transaction—carried a serious responsibility: Uber held the keys to the digital identities of its millions of contractors and customers.

It too often showed it wasn't prepared to shoulder the burden. Back in 2012 Uber published a blog post about how it calculated instances of one-night stands—it called them "rides of glory"—by tabulating rides that terminated late at night, with the same passenger being picked up nearby in the wee hours of the morning. Uber effectively was publicizing the fact that it was analyzing users' data to determine patterns of their sexual activity. "In times of yore you would have woken up in a panic, scrambling in the dark trying to find your fur coat or velvet smoking jacket or whatever it is you cool kids wear," it wrote, bragging about its analytical abilities. "Then that long walk home in the pre-morning dawn. But that was then. The world has changed, and gone are the days of the Walk of Shame. We live in Uber's world now." (It later deleted the blog post.)

Indeed, Uber was surprisingly shortsighted about privacy issues and the potential for its data to be abused. In May 2014, an unknown assailant hacked into Uber's servers and pilfered at least fifty thousand driver names and license numbers from its databases. Uber detected the theft in September, but it wasn't until the following February that it informed its drivers that their personal information had fallen into suspect hands. The breach caused an uproar among Uber's vaunted "partners," especially because the company waited so long to tell them about it. Uber offered affected drivers free credit card security protection. It also said it failed to detect any instances of the data being misused. Nevertheless, the reputational damage was done: Uber was a company that couldn't necessarily be trusted with the data it required its drivers and riders to disclose to it.

Uber also showed signs of being a sneaky steward of such sensitive data. Following the investigation of the data breach, it came to light that Uber maintained a "God view"—later "Heaven view"—tool that enabled employees to track the movement of riders. The existence of this capability in and of itself wasn't shocking. After all, the GPS-enabled technology in its apps allowed riders to see the location of their drivers and to share their expected arrival times with others. What was shocking was how loosely Uber restricted internal access to the tool. When the general manager of the company's New York operation revealed the existence of the tool by telling a journalist he had used it to monitor her, it became apparent that access to the "God view" inside Uber was too broad.

Uber was also implicated in headline-grabbing events that went well beyond creepy. In December 2014, an Uber driver in Delhi was arrested and charged with raping a passenger. Uber was promptly banned in Delhi, and it faced accusations of not having sufficiently vetted the background of the alleged rapist, who at the time was free on bail after having been accused of rape in another part of India. (He was later convicted and sentenced to life in prison.) In India, the high-profile case provoked an outcry over sexual violence. It also put the California company on the hot seat for not having done enough to protect its customers—a charge it would repeatedly face at home too.

With all this going on, Uber needed a single executive to oversee digital and physical safety. This was a tall order among tech companies, which excel at the former but have little experience with the latter. To fill the role, Uber recruited Joe Sullivan, who already was doing the digital aspect of the job for Facebook. Sullivan says he originally wasn't interested, mindful of Uber's dodgy reputation. His Facebook role was satisfying and stimulating, and the prospect of joining a company whose CEO bragged about the babe-magnet qualities of running "Boob-er" weren't appealing. "I was raising three daughters," he said.

What won Sullivan over was the opportunity to oversee "real-world threats and digital threats," to report directly to Kalanick, and to have "relatively unlimited resources" to accomplish his task. His mandate, he says, was to make safety a "brand differentiator" for Uber.

Sullivan entered Uber in the spring of 2015 with a long to-do list. Securing driver and rider data was a matter of adding more rigorous authentication requirements to Uber's account with Amazon Web Services, where Uber stored its data. "We went from basics to best practices," he says. His team researched "telematics," the ability to collect data over networks that measured movement. As an example, Uber's data on how its drivers handle their phones is so precise it can tell if they are holding the phone while driving, a no-no. The company also can tell if drivers are braking too hard or going too fast. Knowing these facts could help Uber be an honest referee when fielding rider complaints. Unruly drunken passengers are a persistent problem for Uber drivers, and Sullivan's team brought a unique physical/digital approach to solving it. "We tested whether distraction and entertainment, like building a game in the app, would help," he says. "We put in detailed bios of drivers to see if it'd build empathy. When you're in a new world, you try new solutions."

It gradually dawned on Uber's leadership that safety was a uniquely physical issue, the "atoms" aspect of Kalanick's "bits and atoms." Sullivan, a cybercrime litigator earlier in his career, had to build up his roster of people who'd worked for companies that physically interacted with consumers on a daily basis, a unique proposition for an "Internet" company. Consumers interacted with Uber drivers around the clock. As well, the company had highly visible driver-support centers in every sizable city, each a potential security risk. "It was much more analogous to running security for McDonald's," says Sullivan. He hired a former secret service agent who'd designed a security regimen for Western Union retail shops. Meeting areas for drivers and riders on the outskirts of major sporting events and concerts required attention too. "The Super Bowl parking lot, for example," Sullivan muses. "There's lots to think about."

As Uber was teaching itself to behave like a big company in how it thought about security and safety, it cranked up a regulatory effort that was bigger than many established companies'. Sally

Kay, a former jazz singer and seamstress in her mid-thirties who got a degree in public policy, had been working in California politics. Immediately before joining Uber she was in the Sacramento office of Del Monte, the food company, working on regulatory affairs. When she joined Uber in the spring of 2014 the company was tracking more than 330 state and local bills in the United States, trying to make sure Uber wasn't regulated out of business. "My favorite thing in going from Del Monte and government to a start-up was how fast things moved," she says. "We were a bunch of happy warriors."

State legislatures are quirky places, often meeting only part time, and 2015 happened to be a big year for Uber because most states were in session. Kay monitored the various jurisdictions where Uber was under attack. A Seattle ordinance, for example, capped "transportation network companies," or TNCs, at one hundred vehicles at a time. Kay worked on legislation in Colorado, which swung from regulation so restrictive it would shut down Uber in Denver to passing one of the first laws that lightly regulated and legalized ridesharing throughout the state. She eventually moved on to Las Vegas, the first city Uber pulled out of and where it eventually won the right to do business—in 2015.

Over and over Uber ran its playbook of soliciting rider and driver support when regulators got in its way. "We won all the time," says Kay, noting that the round-the-clock work "took a toll personally. We were just on one hundred percent, all the time."

Regulatory battles morphed from hair-on-fire crises all the time to sporadic flare-ups, and by 2016 Kalanick began to focus on trying to put the business on a less crisis-oriented, more even-keeled path. Among other things, a company that had been focused on growth at any cost now found it necessary to spend more prudently. "His mantra is to get better at the basics," says David Plouffe. Kalanick's charge in 2016, says Plouffe, was to "improve the apps for both rider and driver, improve the mapping, get better at customer service, and understand that growth is outpacing some of the systems. That was a very mature and a very un-Travis-like thing to do: to slow down is not the right word, but to put a priority on that."

To put systems in place, Kalanick turned to the executive he often tapped for difficult tasks, Austin Geidt. Having risen from intern to head of Uber's city-launch apparatus, Geidt was that rare employee who had relationships throughout the company. She created a team known internally as "PRO," which stands for process resource optimization. It was a kind of management consulting arm inside Uber's walls that made policies, codified best practices, and stamped out inefficiencies. PRO, says Geidt, is "a kind of brain for the company on what's going on." It looked at everything from how to distribute phones to drivers, how to grade analytical tests given to employees, and how to streamline the metrics cities teams around the world use to measure their business. Her task, she says, was to ask: "How do we make Uber a similar experience everywhere? Otherwise this is just going to get really messy."

In some cases, Uber realized it had already become too big. Kalanick would often question why every attendee at meetings needed to be there. He challenged his management team to root out bureaucracy where it wasn't needed. On the East Coast, top operations executive Rachel Holt created a "bureaucracy busters committee" to come up with examples of policies to eliminate. "It was really thinking about how do we continue to move fast, how do we continue to make fast decisions?" she says. As an example, the group decided too few employees had access to a tool to create promotions for their particular market. So they broadened the list. Says Holt: "That was slowing people down."

In other cases, Uber came to the opposite conclusion: it had too little process in place. An example was customer support, which Geidt temporarily took over in mid-2016. "Our support isn't good," she said at the time. "It's frustrating for drivers. It's really frustrating for our riders. And it just isn't aligned with the principles we have set." Geidt began chipping away at the support problems one by one: how and where phone banks were staffed, which calls should be taken by employees and which by contractors, how complaints were routed, and so on. In October the company hired an ex-eBay "customer loyalty" executive named Troy Stevenson to run all support. He knew the challenges well. In his time in between full-time jobs Stevenson had worked part time as an Uber driver. Judging by the persistent complaints from drivers, he continued to have his work cut out for him.

◉──◉

At the same time Uber was trying to get its house in order it was throwing more things against the wall to see what would stick. From nearly the beginning Kalanick had envisioned Uber as more than an improvement on taxis. To him it was a logistics platform capable of moving more than people. If so, what else could Uber pump through its platform, and how could it expand its various money-making ideas to exploit its unique transportation network?

In 2014, Kalanick hired Jason Droege, one of the cofounders of Scour, to a top position at Uber. Whereas many of the original Scour employees had stuck with Kalanick at Red Swoosh or followed Michael Todd to Google, Droege went his own way after Scour's collapse. He founded an online shop to sell used golf equipment called Back 9 Golf. Then he helped start a company called Gizmo5 Technologies, eventually bought by Google, that created an Internet calling service similar to Skype but aimed at small businesses. Next Droege joined Taser International, the stun-gun maker, which had begun selling body cameras to police officers. Droege oversaw a Web-based repository for all the video cops uploaded called Evidence.com.

Droege had discussed working at Uber before, but he decided to see things out at Taser, a publicly traded company in Arizona. He kept in touch with Kalanick, though, and as Uber grew two things dawned on Droege. First, the window was narrowing to move into a significant role at the company, and the opportunity to make a killing by joining at a relatively low valuation was evaporating quickly. More to the point, Kalanick had an opportunity for Droege that matched his eclectic post-Scour background. "He got to the point where he felt like he'd sufficiently focused on the rides business," says Droege. "He had a good team, things were starting to scale. And he wanted to have someone come in and basically work on special projects." Droege's mission was to "go figure out the things that Uber can do that don't involve people transportation" while leveraging Uber's app, customer base, driver network, and presence in cities around the world.

The name for the unit Droege would run grew out of the way entrepreneurs and investors already talked about the opportunities for other businesses to do in their industries what Uber had done in transportation. "People were calling and telling us their ideas for 'Uber for everything,'" says Droege. Nothing was off-limits: Uber for dry cleaning, Uber for house painting, and so on. Droege listened, and he also embarked on a months-long study of what specific projects Uber should pursue. He hit on three, which would be grouped under the corporate catchall label of Uber Everything.

Given its city network, Uber had a powerful method for testing tangential ideas. Each city operated like a small business, more akin to an owned-and-operated affiliate than a branch office, so Uber could seed the concept quietly in a handful of markets to gauge demand. Says Droege: "You can actually run experiments really quickly because the teams on the ground can kind of duct-tape-and-bubble-gum things together to see an idea gets a consumer-demand signal." This is how the three new ideas got going. They were UberEssentials, a service that would deliver convenience-store items (it flopped); UberRush, a business-to-business delivery service that gained traction throughout 2016; and UberEats, a food-delivery service that grew into Uber's second-biggest business after ferrying around people. UberEats began in the spring of 2015 in four cities: Barcelona, Chicago, New York, and Los Angeles. By early 2017 the service operated in sixty-two cities.

Even as Uber was looking for different things to do with its network, it also experimented with offering passengers different options. UberPool is a carpool service that matches riders going similar directions for a dramatically lower fare. (To drivers, UberPool is just another ride, but one with multiple passengers and destinations.) UberCommute, which first operated in Chengdu, in western China, and Chicago, is an attempt to recruit neighbors heading the same direction for work to drive one another and to collect just enough money to defray the costs of commuting— and to pay a slice to Uber. UberHop is a fixed-route, fixed-price service, mimicking the predictability of a bus route but with Uber drivers. Uber ran pilots for UberHop in Seattle (where it charged as little as $1 to ride) and Toronto for much of 2016 before shutting them down, claiming in both cities it had "learned a ton" and would instead apply the lessons learned to UberPool. UberHop still operates in one market, Manila, in the Philippines.

As Uber expanded internationally it tweaked its business with learning from other parts of its empire. Its China unit, for example, offered customers the choice of selecting to ride alone or share a ride when making a request. Choosing to share lowered the fare. Managers in Chicago, a test market for UberPool, decided to try the feature, internally referring to it as the "China toggle." Price comparison of a shared ride with an individual ride became a standard feature where the former was available. In India, Uber's competition allowed cash payments, which Uber did not do. This was close to a religious position for Kalanick, who believed Uber's cashless transactions were part of its secret sauce. Yet India's low credit card adoption slowed Uber's progress, and so the company experimented with accepting cash in one market, the southern city of Hyderabad. Ed Baker, Uber's head of growth strategy, said the dramatic success of the experiment persuaded Kalanick. "He said, 'I hate you guys, but we've got to roll this out.'" Today Uber allows cash payments in multiple Latin American, Asian, and African markets. It even is testing cash transactions in two U.S. cities: Colorado Springs and Denver. Another innovation in the Indian market was UberDost, a stand-alone app that allows drivers to earn bounties for referring friends to become Uber drivers. The app has since expanded globally.

Part of experimenting was also about changing Uber's image. It collaborated with Mothers Against Drunk Driving to encourage young people to take Uber rather than to drive drunk. It created an advisory council of retired generals to encourage military veterans to sign up to drive for Uber. It also partnered with hospitals to make it easier and cheaper for cancer patients returning home after treatments. The posttreatment ride service debuted at the Hackensack Medical Center in New Jersey. Says Rachel Holt, head of North American operations: "These are very different types of partnerships than the black-car-home-from-a-gala type of stuff that we used to do."

Uber took a decentralized approach to such promotions. General managers in particular markets oversaw the outreach to institutions like hospitals. The same was true for the marketing "stunts"—Uber's word for attention-getting ideas like delivering kittens or helicoptering to the Hamptons and highly specific service offerings. Wine regions in San Luis Obispo County, California, and Valle de Guadalupe, Mexico, offered "UberWine" to facilitate wine tours. Offices in New Delhi, Hanoi, and Bangalore were among those to offer UberMoto, rides on the back of a motorcycle. UberBike in cycling-friendly cities like Amsterdam and São Paulo offers the option of choosing drivers with cars outfitted with bike racks.

Local offices were expected to generate their own marketing ideas, and some inevitably proved more annoying than effective. In 2016, the Mexico City office flew Uber-branded drones over cars stuck in traffic, asking in Spanish: "Driving by yourself? This is why you can never see the volcanoes." The message referred to the Mexican capital's view-obscuring smog. The solution: Take UberPool.

Uber was attempting to grow up throughout the company, particularly in its finance function. Having a professional finance group was important because Uber kept on raising money, now at an unprecedented valuation and in amounts never before seen for a traditional venture-capital-backed start-up. By the end of 2016, Uber had raised more than $17 billion, including more than $2 billion of debt. Where once Uber could place representatives from all its venture-capital backers around a conference-room table, now scores of investment groups held stakes, ranging from hedge fund and private-equity firms to mutual funds and sovereign wealth funds. For two of its most formative years, from 2013 to 2015, the company's chief financial officer was Brent Callinicos, a veteran finance executive who had spent years at

Microsoft and then Google. He abruptly stepped down in early 2015, leaving Uber with a team of thirtysomething-year-old former Goldman Sachs bankers in charge of finance and fundraising. Their chief was Gautam Gupta, who while a junior banker at Goldman was part of the team that invested in Uber in 2011.

Uber confounded predictions by the media and market watchers that it would go public quickly. Kalanick repeatedly said the company wasn't in a hurry, and by not replacing Callinicos with a chief financial officer—a prerequisite for an IPO—he proved he meant it. It had become popular among Silicon Valley companies after the dot-com bust to stay private as long as possible. The ability to shield one's finances from competitors was a main reason. Once, companies had used IPOs as a financing event. But companies like Uber didn't need an IPO to raise money.

At the same time, Uber began sharing with investors and prospective investors some of the information it eventually planned to share with securities regulators. It even disclosed its accounting philosophy to the U.S. Securities and Exchange Commission, an unusual practice for a private company. It held quarterly conference calls with investors, exactly as public companies do. "We're trying to operate as professionally as we can," Gupta said in mid-2016, adding that Uber was "close" to being compliant with all the requirements of a public company in the United States. (This refers to adhering to the generally accepted accounting principles and listing requirements that publicly traded companies are required to follow but private companies can skirt.) Says Gupta: "We effectively have all the best practices of a public company, without having a publicly traded stock."

A peek at those numbers reveals why investors were so keen to invest in Uber. For example, in late 2015, when Uber raised money at a valuation of $62.5 billion, its annualized gross bookings were about $13.5 billion, according to someone who had seen the investor presentation. Six months later the annualized pace had grown to $19 billion, a 40 percent uptick. A staple of the Uber investor pitch was its explanation of the "negative churn" it experienced in its mature markets. It shows the percentage of overall users in a given market who use Uber monthly growing over time. If the trend holds—and Uber showed investors how the rider graphs replicated themselves in city after city—it demonstrates how riders use Uber more over time, making the service more efficient as it grows. "Churn" refers to the rate at which users abandon a service. By demonstrating that usage picked up velocity over time, Uber demonstrated the opposite of churn. "We see that phenomenon in pretty much every city around the world, whether it's London, Sydney, LA, New York, Delhi, Beijing," said Uber's Gupta (before Uber abandoned China). "We see that everywhere."

Financial analysts refer to this method of comparing multiple markets at similar stages of development as "cohort analysis." Uber showed investors that its earliest customer "cohort" in San Francisco grew over the course of three years from using Uber about two times a month to fifteen times. "This is the oldest cohort," says Gupta. "You see the same phenomenon around the world. If you look at every other single cohort, they formulate the same pattern." What makes the analysis relevant is that by sharing the data with investors and making the claim that it followed a predictable trajectory, Uber allowed investors to build their own financial models for Uber's future. This is what led investors to bid up the company's valuation.

By opening for business in hundreds of cities around the world, Uber was also able to show its investors the expected path to profitability in each market. "On day one we can't keep drivers busy all the time," explains Gupta. "So we actually buy their supply hours. We are guaranteeing them income. That goes on for nine to ten months or so in a given city. So we are actually making a loss in every city that we're launching. That's what we call incubating a city, where the investment is made to make sure that the drivers are out there whenever a rider opens the app." Gupta says that as Uber builds critical mass in a city, the volume of rides drives a virtuous cycle of efficiency, enabling Uber to eliminate the guarantees and become profitable. By early 2016 Uber was profitable in 108 cities, about a fourth of the total.

If investment hurt potential profitability, competition was a much bigger problem. During the first week of 2016 Uber's primary competitor in the United States, Lyft, announced a partnership with and investment by General Motors. GM agreed to invest $500 million, with plans to build its self-driving car capacity on the strength of Lyft's national network. Lyft gave GM a seat at the technology table. GM provided Lyft with money, which it promptly began using to take market share from Uber in crucial markets, including San Francisco and Los Angeles. Lyft's market share in major markets typically had been around 20 percent. In early 2016, with Uber attempting to squeeze costs out of its operations, Lyft began taking share, growing its share to as much as 37 percent, by Uber's calculations, in San Francisco.

With similar products, market share was simply a function of price. The service that offered cheaper rides to consumers and bigger bounties to drivers gained more business. Uber, which had been profitable in its U.S. business in the last quarter of 2015, had a problem on its hands. "We then had to make a conscious decision to forgo profitability in a city like San Francisco to gain market share back," says Gupta. By midyear, Uber had reduced Lyft's share in the headquarters city they shared from 37 percent to 30 percent. Uber referred to this as a "balance sheet war," and its balance sheet, with $5 billion at the time, was considerably bigger than Lyft's.

At the end of the day, Uber moves to the occasionally eccentric and frequently capricious beat of its CEO, who sometimes inspires and quite often infuriates even his most loyal acolytes. To watch Uber mature is to see a CEO sometimes at war with himself over competing impulses: the need to build a modern corporation versus the desire to run a scrappy, nimble, and convention-defying start-up. Says Geidt: "I think in his head he's like, 'Make it hum while you're innovating and breaking things.'" Geidt sees a "tension" in Kalanick, who still wants to experiment while being mindful of the need for prudence. There was a time, she says, when she and others had a blank check so long as they were building the company. "Now," she says, "we have these tedious budget meetings, which have to happen. We're fighting for every head." She says Kalanick can be sorely tempted to abet her desire to go around the finance department while still urging her to prove the value of a plan. "We want to go public someday," says Geidt. "We really do. And so, everyone doesn't just get the blank check we used to. Travis really does try to balance all of it. There is a lot more talk when I want to experiment about proving the ROI first."

In his heart, Kalanick will always be more entrepreneur than administrator. "He wants everything to happen at once," says Geidt. "And I'll say, 'Okay, that doesn't make sense.' But as a result we have to juggle the impossible. I think he's always going to push to innovate, disrupt, do more. There is never a day when he's like, 'Oh, this is perfect, let's just stay on this trajectory.'"

Like the cohort of "visionary" CEOs with whom he identifies, Kalanick is a sponge for new concepts. Yet he's also a born spit-baller, and his desire to act on his impulses can scramble the best-laid plans. "He'll call me and say, 'Hey, I have a crazy idea,' and whenever he does that, I'm like, 'No,' because he always starts so far out," says Geidt. "I say, 'We can't do that, that's crazy.' But then we find a middle ground." Or, more likely, his minions simply do what Kalanick asks. Kalanick recently met a prominent Pakistani at an event hosted by Eric Schmidt, executive chairman of Google parent Alphabet as well as a personal investor in Uber. Kalanick phoned Geidt shortly afterward and pronounced, "Lahore. We've got to be in Lahore." Within months, Uber was operating in Pakistan's second-largest city.

So long as you don't work for him, Kalanick's rat-a-tat-tat idea generation can be highly entertaining. Toward the end of a long dinner, Kalanick once pitched me a nutty concept involving my own business, the media industry. Fed up by his negative press, he imagined a news organization with high-quality journalists who wrote articles commissioned by their corporate subjects, like Uber. The client wouldn't dictate the direction of articles or otherwise interfere with the reporting of an article. But it would have the option to kill the article. He knew he was fighting an uphill battle with me and that no amount of beer would soften my disdain for his idea. I later shared this anecdote with Geidt, who responded with a sort of knowing ennui. "He has them all the time," she said. "But sometimes he's right. Oftentimes I've got to be the voice of reason. He does have an inner circle where he'll lean on us to greenlight something, and if one of us says no, he'll go to the next person until he gets someone to sign off on it. But it has made us all better. He starts out there, and it's exhausting because it's like, 'No, don't you dare do that. We're not doing that.' But it has certainly driven us to be where we are now."

CHAPTER 9
Driver's Seat

When I decided to write this book I knew it would be a good idea to do at least a short stint as an Uber driver. Though a bit apprehensive that I'd be any good at it, I was excited by the opportunity. Rarely does a business journalist get a chance to do the work of the company he covers. I can't write code for Google, and Apple is unlikely to hire me to hawk iPhones in its retail stores. But almost anyone can drive for Uber, and so for once I could get a worm's-eye view of the company I was trying to understand.

I'll bet like a lot of other people, I also had a romantic notion of what it'd be like to drive a taxi. I used to brag that my job as a journalist in Chicago gave me a street-level knowledge of that great city, one that was equal to a cabbie's. But I knew that wasn't true. Only by driving a city's streets for hours on end and interacting with its inhabitants and visitors could one truly know it.

And I'd never had the time or sufficient interest to drive a cab. Still, the idea of it appealed, and now was my chance to do something similar.

In fact, this wasn't my first brush with driving for Uber. Back in 2010, when Uber was just getting going, I talked to the company about becoming a chauffeur as part of an article I'd write in *Fortune.* (A confession: I very likely was motivated by the prospect of a photo of myself in the magazine wearing a black chauffeur's cap. I can't articulate why that excited me. But it did.) Uber at the time was a black-car service only, and the hoops I was asked to jump through before getting behind the wheel are telling, especially in hindsight. For example, it wasn't possible simply to sign up and become an Uber driver then. Only licensed and insured limousine drivers with access to a suitable vehicle were eligible. Uber, then a young company eager for publicity, offered to connect me with one of the limo services it had recruited to its network, 7x7 Executive Transportation in San Francisco. 7x7 would take me on as a driver for one weekend and would temporarily add my name to its insurance policy.

Getting going promised to be arduous. For starters, Uber e-mailed me some advice. A company representative suggested that I familiarize myself with San Francisco, "either by driving around or studying maps." (Maps!) I also would be required to take a drug test. Then I would have to schedule an hour-and-a-half-long "onboarding" appointment with an Uber trainer. And I'd have to sit for a written test and interview that would take about an hour.

Regrettably, I never became an Uber limo driver. Shortly after beginning my dialogue with the start-up in the fall of 2010, my time got sucked up by more pressing projects, including completing a book about the inner workings of Apple. My notes from the abortive experiment would become instructive down the road, however.

Fast forward to the spring of 2016, when I began my second quest to write about joining Uber's ranks. First I would need a car, having assumed that my 2002 Nissan Pathfinder was too old for the job, which some time before I had read on Uber's Web site was the case. I considered leasing, renting, or financing a car through one of the services Uber provides its drivers. But when I sat down at my computer near lunchtime on a sunny day in late May to investigate, I learned that my fourteen-year-old car, with nearly 100,000 miles on it, was eligible after all. (Over time, Uber has significantly loosened the restrictions on the age of the cars drivers could use in an effort to boost driver rolls.) It took about fifteen minutes to input my driver's license and to give Uber permission to conduct a criminal background check on me. And that was it.

Next I got up from my desk and drove to Uber's San Francisco inspection center, which happens to be in my neighborhood. There was no wait to be seen. An Uber employee gave my car a cursory once-over. (Seat belts? Check. Taillights? Check. Done.) Then another Uber employee verified my auto insurance and vehicle registration, helped me download the rider app onto my phone, and issued me a permit to display in my window when I picked up or dropped off at local airports. I got a welcome packet with Uber logo stickers to put in my front and back windows. Nearby lurked a man working for a car-cleaning service. He handed me a flyer and told me to call him when a passenger vomited in my backseat. The implication was that this was a matter of when, not if.

And I was done. From the moment I registered online to when I thanked the cheerful Uber worker who handed me my welcome packet about an hour had passed. I was soon informed by text message that my background check would take up to five business days. It took three, and by the following week I was a full-fledged Uber driver. Drug tests aren't required to drive your own car. Studying maps was a thing of the past: the app would guide me with turn-by-turn directions. Adjusting my insurance to commercial status, if that's what I chose to do, was my problem, not Uber's. I needed no additional license as I wasn't technically becoming a professional driver. There was no test, no interview, no nothing—at least not beyond the helpful (and unofficial) advice of what to do when a drunken reveler became sick in my backseat. I was ready to turn on my Uber driver app and start making money.

Getting going really was that easy. When I opened the Uber driver app for the first time I was encouraged to watch a video with tips for new drivers. It urged me to ask my passengers their names to verify I was collecting the right person. It gave me advice on being polite as a way of giving good service—and getting a good rating.

I was intent on making a good impression, and so the first thing I did was get my car washed. Then I bought a cooler full of small bottles of water, which I kept in my front seat and offered to each customer. Alas, not one rider accepted my water, though perhaps they appreciated the gesture: to this day my Uber driver rating is a perfect five stars.

Clean car and cool beverages aside, I was a beginner, and I knew it—because I drove around for the next hour without getting a fare. Any experienced driver would have known that mid-morning in a residential neighborhood of San Francisco was no time or place to get rides. I also hadn't yet mastered how to read the driver app's surge-pricing heat map, which shows drivers where they can make the most money.

Instinct told me to drive downtown in the late afternoon, and sure enough I got my first request from Daniel, a college student at the University of Arizona just completing his first day of a summer internship at the jobs-site company LinkedIn. I picked him up at 4:18 P.M.—why was he leaving work so early on his first day?—and took him to an apartment in a neighborhood called the Inner Sunset, where he was sharing a room for the summer. I was fortunate that my first customer could not have been nicer, even as I fumbled with how to correctly work the app and made a couple wrong turns.

The nearly five-mile trip, from the heart of San Francisco's central business district to the perennially foggy neighborhood near Golden Gate Park, lasted twenty-two minutes. Daniel and I chatted about his internship experience and what he hoped to do when he graduated from college. I told him about the summer camps my daughter was attending. I was extremely aware of the incongruity of my being a college-educated middle-aged man driving around a college kid who thought nothing of hailing a ride home rather than taking public transportation. He seemed to give the situation no thought one way or the other.

Thanks to the mapping software in the Uber app—drivers could choose from Google Maps, Waze (which Google owns), or an Uber-owned mapping product—I easily found Daniel's summer digs. (Turn-by-turn directions, with destination information inputted by the customer, have rendered local knowledge and even command of the local language unnecessary; I once was driven around San Francisco by a young woman who had recently arrived from China and spoke almost no English: her navigation system talked to her in Chinese.) After dropping Daniel I pulled over to see how much I had earned and to figure out what to do next. A more experienced driver would simply keep rolling, the better to find his next ride, but I wanted to see the fruits of my labor. The fare for my first trip was $12.22. After deducting Uber's 25 percent commission, or $3.06, I was left with $9.16 for a little less than a half hour of work. (My $12 car wash and $9.99 case of bottled water meant I was still in the hole.) I was also out of position, as I now would have to head back toward a busier section of town for my next ride, which I found twenty-five unproductive minutes later near San Francisco's City Hall.

This time my passengers were two twentysomething tech workers who discussed a meeting they had just completed and were heading to one or the other's apartment to continue working. I don't know anything more about them because they ignored me completely, something I've done countless times with my Uber and taxi drivers. That one-mile ride lasted a mere six minutes, and the passenger who exited from the right side of my vehicle neglected to close the door all the way but was long gone before I could get his attention. I had to pull over past the next traffic light to get out of my car to close it. The fare for that trip was $5, leaving me with $3.75 after Uber's commission. It was already dawning on me that this was an exceedingly difficult way to make a living, making me more empathetic to the people who do it. I decided to switch off the driver app and head home for dinner.

I drove a few more times in order to satisfy my curiosity about the challenges Uber drivers face. One day I took a Brazilian software executive and avid sailor to the airport, where I picked up a management consultant from Dallas and delivered him to a downtown meeting. I told both why I was driving for Uber, and they seemed intrigued. That same day I picked up a mother and daughter with a huge suitcase, which I put in the back of my SUV. Like cabbies everywhere I excitedly assumed we were going to the airport. We weren't. They were only going to breakfast a mile away. One morning I picked up a smartly dressed young woman who lives two blocks from my home and who very likely is an investment banker because the building where I dropped her downtown has quite a few investment banks. I don't know for sure what she does because she barely said a word to me. Instead, she silently studied her iPhone for the entire ride. (My take: $6.08.)

I tried to have at least a little fun with my temporary chauffeur gig. One summer morning I drove my wife and daughter downtown, the former to work and the latter to day camp. My wife hailed me by sitting in the passenger seat at my side and requesting a ride as soon as I turned on the driver app. (As I was the closest available driver it was a near certainty the algorithm would choose me.) The two people I love most in the world proceeded to criticize my driving for the entire trip—this wasn't unusual—but in a shameless example of grade padding, I implored my wife to give me five stars. (She did.) That trip cost my wife $9.71, meaning that we paid Uber $2.43 for the privilege of conducting our research experiment.

I can't pretend I ever mastered the art of driving for Uber. Learning all the tricks like chasing surge-pricing areas, taking advantage of periodic incentives, figuring out how to navigate the airport, staying away from areas where you're most likely to have your backseat covered in vomit—those take time. What's more, the low-grade stress of driving around strangers, not being paid attention to, and being stuck in traffic on someone's else's schedule all made me appreciate my day job that much more. There's no doubt the flexibility of being an Uber driver is attractive. But the pay stinks, and the work is difficult. I'll happily stick with journalism.

◉—————————————————————————————◉

Harry Campbell is an unlikely spokesman for Uber drivers of the world. A lanky thirty-year-old native of Los Angeles, he graduated from Santa Monica High School, studied aerospace engineering at the University of California, San Diego, and worked during his twenties as a structural engineer for two aircraft makers, including Boeing. He was making a comfortable, six-figure salary, putting his education to good use. Yet he wasn't satisfied. "I by no stretch hated those jobs, but I wasn't super passionate about them," he tells me over lunch in Manhattan Beach, a tony community near Los Angeles International Airport and not far from Campbell's current home in Long Beach. "I just wasn't excited to go to work on Monday."

What was getting Campbell excited was what he calls his "side hustle," a trendy expression associated with the so-called gig economy that once would have been called moonlighting. He was intrigued by personal finance, suddenly having some considerable disposable income, and so in 2012 he started a blog targeted at people like himself. It's called *Your Personal Finance Pro*, with the tagline "Financial Advice for Young Professionals." The blog was a small-scale success and generated good income for Campbell, nearly a couple thousand dollars a month for not very much effort. Campbell realized he immensely enjoyed the direct payoff blogging delivered, especially compared with his staid salaried job. "It was like, oh, man, I did that, I created that," he says. "I think that's a really cool feeling that a lot of people underestimate."

Then, in 2014, Campbell discovered Uber. He already knew he liked making extra cash after hours by indulging a personal interest, and he thought he might try driving for the service. Immediately, he says, "a natural lightbulb went off in my head." Not only could he experiment with this newfangled idea whose novelty appealed to him, he could write about it too. "I signed up for these services, and I went out and just did it one night and I was like, man, this isn't rocket science. But there's a lot more to it than you'd expect. It's not as simple as just picking up someone at Point A and then dropping him off in Orange County." It was a time when many of the rules of engagement for drivers were still being figured out. "There was a lot of crazy stuff going on at that time, with you having to do airport rides, which were basically illegal, and you could potentially get fined," Campbell reflects. "But Uber was telling you to do it."

In other words, it was frontier days in a new industry, and Campbell would become the equivalent of the newspaperman in a gold-rush town. He started a new blog, *The Rideshare Guy*, and he quickly became the analytical yet passionate voice of independent-contractor drivers everywhere. Campbell started by writing about his own experiences as a driver, particularly for Uber, but also for competing services like Lyft and DoorDash and any other company pursuing a similar business model. He was bullish on the field, considering that he liked the independence and freshness of it. But he was also an unbiased and critical voice in a burgeoning space. "I would go out and detail—in pretty detailed spreadsheets, because I'm an engineer—how much money I was making and breaking it down by hour, by ride; how much time I'm sitting with a passenger, without a passenger, and so on," he says. He became an advocate for Uber drivers, many of whom criticize the company for treating them like numbers rather than people. "I basically gave a very realistic point of view. There's definitely good things about it. But there's this whole laundry list of challenges. Like, have you ever tried to e-mail Uber for help? They don't know what they're doing."

What started as a writing project became a business built on filling in the holes of Uber's cobbled-together offering. Where Uber offered a cursory video on its driver app—the one I watched in a few minutes before beginning to drive—*The Rideshare Guy* offers a comprehensive video training program for $97. Uber gives its drivers minimal instruction on how to obtain auto insurance. Campbell runs an online marketplace for agents to hawk their services. And he sells advertising space to small-business-oriented vendors who want to reach drivers. These include established players that cater to freelancers, like Quick-Books Self-Employed, the bookkeeping software owned by Silicon Valley giant Intuit. As well, Campbell's advertisers include a grab bag of vendors that, like his blog, have formed a new economy around Uber and similar companies. San Francisco's Stride Drive, for example, offers drivers an app to track their mileage as well as expenses like health care, car washes, parking, and tolls. DailyPay is a New York start-up that cashes out drivers on a daily basis.

The Rideshare Guy's steadiest source of revenue is derived from the drumbeat of new drivers for Uber, Lyft, and other services. As Campbell's blog is the go-to source for information about driving for Uber, anyone trying to learn the ropes checks it out. Despite having become too busy to drive much because of the demands of his business, Campbell maintains his active status by going on the occasional run, enabling him to collect the bounties all the services offer drivers for referring newbies. Says Campbell: "I put my code up there"—on his site—"so when people sign up, or they're researching, they can use my code to sign up, and I get a bonus."

No subject is too arcane for Campbell. He'll analyze every angle for making money off Uber and its competitors. He advises readers on when to drive for which service, by playing them off against each other depending on who is offering better incentives.

He helps with pesky topics like car maintenance, insurance, tax preparation, and the like. And he serves as a one-man complaint line: unlike Uber, he answers every e-mail he receives, putting him in a unique position to understand what is and isn't working at Uber. In fact, Campbell estimates he has communicated directly with more than thirty thousand drivers over three years via e-mail, social media, and in person.

Uber keeps a close eye on Campbell. "They pay very careful attention to what I'm doing," he says. "And so I've taken meetings with them. Last time I went to San Francisco, I met with them and tried to help them understand what drivers want and what drivers need." Being brought inside Uber's corporate offices has been illuminating. "Once you get in there, they do have a lot of people working on driver-friendly stuff. It just doesn't always come across when you're staring at the app as a driver. So it's important for me to get both sides of the story. Even though I'm running the site for drivers, I still want to hear what Uber has to say about all these things that I'm complaining about." It turns out Uber is as interested in Campbell as he is in them. "They're always telling me, 'Hey, we want to know what things we should change.' And then they actually go out and change them, especially when the changes reflect Uber's priorities." Campbell isn't paid by Uber, other than the new-driver referrals he collects for sending readers their way. In fact, he's providing the company a free service. Reflecting on one visit in San Francisco, he says, "I'd say they really got their money's worth because I met with nineteen different people."

Given his mastery of the driver perspective, Campbell has a

take on all the important debates involving Uber. In 2016 a federal judge in San Francisco overturned an agreement by Uber and Lyft with their drivers in California and Massachusetts that would have seen Uber paying out $100 million to confirm the drivers' status as independent contractors. The original settlement had been a victory for Uber, which wants to avoid paying its drivers as employees. (Employees demand benefits and earn minimum wages.) Campbell sees both sides of the argument. "Obviously as a true independent contractor, you wouldn't take jobs where you're going to lose money," he says, noting that Uber's rules require drivers to accept assignments if they don't want to lose out on potential bonuses or face "timeouts" when they are blocked from using the app. "Uber benefits a lot from that. If you're out in the middle of nowhere and you request a ride, you probably should have to pay more than someone who's in the middle of the city, right? I mean it's kind of like simple free market economics. But with Uber, that driver has to go out there and pick you up, which creates a great service—for the passenger. It's just not a true independent contractor model. I'm also a realist. I know that the platform wouldn't work if drivers could cherry-pick their rides. Then they'd be just like taxis. But I think that drivers should have some say."

Over time Uber has lowered its prices as well as the commissions it pays drivers. It has argued that because its system has become more efficient, overall driver pay hasn't gone down. (Busier drivers should earn the same as higher-paid, more idle drivers, Uber contends.) Campbell doesn't buy it. "I've never met a single driver who's e-mailed me and said, 'Man, I'm making way more now that prices are lower,'" he says. Uber, he says, is good at picking the numbers that fit the story it wants to tell. "In the past they would say, 'Hey, our drivers in New York make $90,000 a year. That's more than a taxicab.' But they don't take into account expenses, and the taxis do. So it's like apples to oranges."

Campbell's primary beef with Uber is that despite its corporate line of calling drivers its "customers," the company puts passengers first. His driver focus is a helpful corrective to the predominant narratives about Uber, be they about its business, its fund-raising, or its regulatory battles. *The Rideshare Guy* has gotten big enough that Campbell now has writers working for him. One, John Ince, wrote a critique of an onstage interview Travis Kalanick did in late 2016 with Graydon Carter, the editor of the magazine *Vanity Fair*. "The interview is revealing not because of what Kalanick says," Ince writes. "What's revealing is how insulated Kalanick comes across. Somebody who seems to have no consciousness of that big elephant standing over there in the corner—driver dissatisfaction. No mention of the safety thing, no awareness of the stark conditions that exist for most drivers, no awareness of the toil and the frustrations of the drivers. Instead he's talking about big concept issues, as he must because these are the issues that *his* people want to hear about. His people, of course, are the investors, the analysts, the lawyers, and the media reps who have come together to make the Uber phenomenon one of the most fascinating stories of the entire decade."

For his part, Campbell is a born critic, but also a grateful one. "I'm very thankful they came up with this business model," he says, likening his outfit to a credit agency that wouldn't exist without Uber but isn't beholden to it either. "It allowed me to quit my job, start my own business that's been very successful, hire people, and work from home. I mean, it has really changed my life."

No two Uber drivers have the same story, though patterns develop the more you talk to them. They like the flexibility, but the hours are long if they want to hit their financial targets. Pay rates have gone down over time. Uber's customer service isn't very good. Riders tip too infrequently. Aside from the truly part time, those who are looking for an interesting diversion or to make some spending money, most have come to the same conclusion I did: driving for Uber is a tough way to make a living.

All drivers have their tactics. Todd Snover, a contract photographer in Omaha, drives around ten hours a week, often traveling as far as Lincoln, more than fifty miles down Interstate 80, to ferry University of Nebraska Cornhusker football fans. Snover has a strict policy for deciding when to drive. "I don't drive if it's not surging." A ridesharing driver since 2015—he also drives for Lyft—Snover has been able to track the decline in Uber payments. He says he earned about $1.50 per mile when he started out. That rate dropped to $1.20 and then a mere 90 cents, which explains his surge-only practice. On the other hand, Snover deftly learned how to take advantage of the generous incentives Uber and Lyft have paid to build up their driver rolls. He said he got $500 for signing up his wife to drive for each service. Together with minimum-level bonuses, the two banked $1,400 from Uber and Lyft just for starting to drive.

Many Uber drivers also follow a predictable path from

excitement to disappointment to resignation. Bineyam Tesfaye, a former cabbie in Washington, D.C., started driving for Uber in 2016 and was pleased to be earning up to $1,200 a week. He earned about that in his best weeks driving a cab in Richmond, Virginia, before that business got zapped by ridesharing. Driving for Uber is harder than operating a taxi, says Tesfaye. Before, he could wait for passengers at a cab stand, giving him time to stretch and chat with other drivers. Now, to hit his goals, his car must always be in motion, and his days are longer. "The constant driving, wear and tear on vehicle and body is pretty insane," he said. Like so many others, he grumbles about the 25 percent commission he pays Uber, even while he's responsible for maintaining his car. "Drivers are working way more, for way less, and Uber is building this giant company," he says.

Because Uber is so dominant, it typically offers the most opportunity to drivers. More customers means more trips, which means greater financial prospects. But Uber seems incapable of perfecting its customer service, at least to the satisfaction of drivers trying to make a living on its platform. Mark Lewandoske, a retired naval officer living near San Diego, figures his military service is his edge with customers in an area with plenty of active-duty personnel and veterans. There is a feature in the Uber app that allows vets like Lewandoske to identify themselves as veterans, but riders aren't seeing his badge. He has sent multiple e-mails to Uber customer service. "They respond that the issue is resolved," he says. "It's not resolved until I say it's resolved." He keeps driving, though. And he confesses that Uber reminds him of the military in one way. "It's the turn-by-turn navigator that's the drill sergeant now," he says.

CHAPTER 10

The Autonomous Future

One of the most important jobs of any business leader is to stay abreast of factors that could disrupt their comfortable status quo. This might be new competitors. It could be new segments of the market their company doesn't currently serve. Unanticipated shifts in consumer attitudes or behavior could be downright devastating. Any one of these factors can destroy an incumbent business or industry. But no factor disrupts the status quo more than technology. Innovation renders entire industries obsolete, so much so that timeworn metaphors describe the impact. The internal combustion engine ransacked the horse-and-buggy industry so thoroughly that it became a cautionary tale for any business whose need for being all but ceases.

Uber, of course, quickly threatened to equate taxis with the horse-and-buggy trade. The start-up had, to reach for another technological cliché, built a better mousetrap, one that relied on a machine in one critical function rather than a person. That entailed designing a superior ride request fulfillment system—a GPS-enabled smartphone that trumped a surly radio dispatcher—as well as a more efficient business model. Uber, after all, never invested a nickel in a fleet of cars. And in the one area where humans were critical to deliver service, Uber barely needed to manage its volunteer army of drivers.

In the summer of 2013, with his business booming yet barely three years old, Travis Kalanick confronted Uber's own potential disruption: autonomous vehicles, also known as self-driving cars. The development was so potentially game-changing that it could eliminate the one area where Uber still relied on people. These vehicles would use rapid advancement of sensors and artificial intelligence to "see" all the obstacles and guideposts that drivers need to navigate. In theory, autonomous vehicles would be far safer, given that robots aren't susceptible to drowsiness or distraction. While radical, there was ample precedent for the technology. In aviation, the autopilot for decades had played a role in dramatically reducing airplane fatality rates. The other advantage to robots, of course, is that they are cheaper than people. Uber pays as much as 75 cents of every dollar it collects to human drivers. This unruly lot complains, often loudly; stops to eat and satisfy other biological necessities; and more than occasionally has unsatisfactory interactions with paying customers. Uber's business would be that much better if only it could eliminate the nuisance of a human workforce.

Deploying robots was more than a cost-savings opportunity for Uber, however. Given the global infrastructure it had built around human drivers, autonomous vehicles represented an existential threat. If other companies developed the technology first and either offered their own services to compete with Uber or licensed the technology at too steep a price, Uber could be every bit as disrupted as the taxi industry was by Uber. This all felt quaintly futuristic in 2013. Still, the one company that could trounce Uber by creating a taxi-like service was already developing a self-driving car, seemingly on a whim. It was a tech powerhouse with vast resources that had already created one of the best digital street-mapping systems in the world. And that company, Google, was on the verge of making a major investment in Uber.

And yet, these were still early days for self-driving cars. The concept largely resided in the labs of robotics departments of engineering schools. When Kalanick was first able to check under the hood of Google's autonomous program, he wasn't the least bit impressed. In preparation for a meeting with Google CEO Larry Page, Kalanick was invited to take a ride in one of Google's self-driving cars, which were tooling around the company's Mountain View, California, campus. Such rides had become a staple for visiting dignitaries, kind of like a trip to the Great Wall of China or a stroll down the empty street of a movie set. If you were important enough, you were offered a ride in a Google self-driving car. It took more than razzle-dazzle to impress Kalanick, however, and for all the gee-whiz promise of Google's bold technological experiment, he was underwhelmed. "The car barely worked," he says of his experience. "At times it would do some things it was supposed to. And other times it wouldn't. It was just not there yet."

Google's kludgy performance reminded Kalanick, a tough

critic but also a careful student of technology history, of an earlier groundbreaking advancement he'd witnessed. A decade earlier he'd been asked to participate at a tech-industry trade show
on a panel on voice-recognition software. "Before I went on the
panel, I did a bunch of research on voice recognition," he says. "I
went on the trade floor, and I met all these dudes, all the companies doing voice recognition. It was like high hopes. But this stuff
was nowhere near ready for prime time. And that was 2000.
That's what driverless felt like in '13. It felt super early." He says
no lightbulb went off in his head signaling that Google's technology was something that could affect Uber. "I mean, it was interesting and cool," he says, but no more. "But," Kalanick adds, "things
move faster these days."

Indeed, the show-and-tell session at Google made enough of
an impression that Kalanick began chatting up friends and colleagues about how quickly the technology might develop. Kalanick had one pal who was better placed than almost anyone to help
him understand why Uber needed to take autonomous vehicles
seriously. This was Sebastian Thrun, the German roboticist who
launched Google's autonomous efforts. Thrun had been a robotics professor at Carnegie Mellon University, home to some of the
most advanced research on machine learning and artificial intelligence, when a research arm of the Pentagon started a competition to develop driverless cars. The so-called DARPA Grand
Challenge was a bid by the Defense Advanced Research Projects
Agency to encourage academics to help the U.S. military field a
fighting force that relied less on putting soldiers in harm's way.
Between the time of the first challenge and the third, in 2005,

Thrun had abandoned CMU in Pittsburgh for the sunnier climes of Stanford University, in the heart of Silicon Valley. His research team there won the DARPA competition, beating out a team from CMU, which took second place.

Google's founders, all-but-dissertation former computer scientists themselves, were part of a Silicon Valley coterie of technologists who loved such competitions. They rejoiced in the XPRIZE competition to build a privately funded spacecraft, for example. (Larry Page would join the XPRIZE Foundation's board of trustees.) And they knew their technology history: it was DARPA's predecessor, ARPA, which sponsored the research that created the Internet, the basis for their fortunes. So suffice it to say they paid keen attention to scientific breakthrough prizes that engaged the computer science departments from which they continued to recruit as well as the government agency that sponsored the competitions.

Several years after the DARPA Grand Challenge, Larry Page and Sergey Brin decided they wanted to build a self-driving car. Never mind that it had little to do with Google's information-quest mission. It was "moonshot" technology they wanted to advance. They persuaded Thrun to leave Stanford in 2010 to help start an in-house research arm called Google X. The group would go on to develop diverse technology such as antiaging drugs and computers that could be printed on eyeglasses and contact lenses. Its first project would be a self-driving car.

Thrun helped develop software called Street View and sent cars driven by Google engineers onto city streets to map everything from street signs to the placement of barriers. Google also bought a small company called 510 Systems, founded by an engineer named Anthony Levandowski, that specialized in self-driving technology. The Google effort was a classic skunk works project: a seemingly goofy, behind-the-scenes science experiment that Google trotted out for the public often enough to get a positive public-relations glow.

In 2013, however, Thrun dropped out of the self-driving car game by leaving Google to start a completely different venture, the online education company Udacity. He committed to remaining a Google adviser for two years, effectively keeping him away from working with any other self-driving car entity. At the same time, he and Kalanick saw each other socially, and the subject of autonomous vehicles was a frequent topic of conversation. "Travis started asking me a lot of questions," says Thrun. "He became very concerned that self-driving taxis were a threat to Uber. It became clear to me he was quite paranoid."

Kalanick's paranoia was justified. While several auto companies were playing with the idea of adding autopilot-like functionality to normal passenger-driven cars, Google decided that only by eliminating the steering wheel altogether would traffic accidents be decreased dramatically. (Humans taking control in an emergency negated the safety gains from automation.) Unlike other companies, Google didn't try particularly hard to hide what it was up to. In mid-2014 it released a video about its self-driving efforts that made it plain that although its venture arm had invested more than $250 million in Uber and one of its top executives had joined Uber's board, Google had Uber in its sights. One application of its wholly automated car, Google said, was a smartphone app that could summon and direct driverless taxis. By this time, Travis Kalanick was paying careful attention.

The same executive Kalanick asked to revamp product development would be his liason to the advent of self-driving cars. Jeff Holden, a wiry computer scientist with a face reminiscent of Howdy Doody and a mile-a-minute style of talking, was a rare talent in the technology world, having begun his career as a protégé of Jeff Bezos, the founder of Amazon. Holden studied computer science at the University of Illinois and then landed after college on Wall Street rather than Silicon Valley. He worked for a hedge fund called D. E. Shaw, which specialized in computer-aided trading strategies. His boss there was Bezos, a computer whiz at Princeton just a few years Holden's senior.

When Bezos left D. E. Shaw to start Amazon, Holden waited two years to follow him, as Bezos had promised not to recruit internally.

Holden would do two things at Amazon that would prepare him well for Uber. First, he built Amazon's supply-chain "optimization" system, the massively complex computer-driven network that whizzes products from warehouse shelves to consumer doorsteps. Next he ran what Amazon calls consumer applications, all the technology that makes shopping at Amazon work, including site search, personalization, the much-copied shopping cart, and so on. Holden left Amazon in 2006 to start a shopping site that the online commerce company Groupon bought in

2011. Groupon, a Chicago company that briefly was worth more than $30 billion but didn't have the good sense to sell when Google offered to buy it, was fizzling by the time Kalanick came calling.

Kalanick visited Holden in Chicago in early 2014 in the dead of winter, before Holden started at Uber. Not for the first time, Kalanick wasn't prepared for the weather: he had neglected to bring an overcoat for a trip to the Midwest. Recalls Holden: "We wanted to go out and get dinner, and I told him, 'You can't actually walk like that. You will be dead by the time we get to the restaurant.' So I gave him a coat. That's a classic Travis thing."

Once inside where it was warm, Holden and Kalanick got down to discussing Holden's product ideas. "I had created a list of something like seventy-four ideas for Uber, and we were going through that list," says Holden. "When self-driving came up, I said, 'Let me pause you there because I have a pretty good view on this.'" Holden says Kalanick hadn't thought deeply on the topic yet but that he understood self-driving cars were inevitable. "We obviously want to participate in that because it will happen with or without us," Kalanick told Holden, who then challenged his soon-to-be boss. "I said, 'I totally agree with you. The problem is it's also a disruption wave in our rearview mirror.'" This surprised Kalanick. After all, he'd been uninspired the previous summer during his visit to Google. Holden says Kalanick judged self-driving cars to be ten to fifteen years away. "I told him it's going to come faster than people think and it's also going to be proprietary."

The point about autonomous car technology being proprietary was jarring. "It's not going to be something like an open self-driving alliance that's going to provide fantastic self-driving software that anybody can use," Holden argued. He told Kalanick that whoever had consumer reach, capital, and the right technology would become "the Uber of the future." Holden hadn't started work yet, but already he was making a dire prediction. "They can leapfrog us and basically replace Uber with a self-driving version of Uber," Holden said.

Holden joined Uber in February 2014, and together with an engineer named Matt Sweeney, he spent his first six months canvassing the world for robotics talent. They studied the teams that had competed in another DARPA competition, the DARPA Urban Challenge, and then they set out to meet as many people as they could. Three academic centers emerged as fertile hunting grounds for the type of robotics talent that would lend itself to autonomous vehicles: MIT, Oxford, and Carnegie Mellon, the school where Sebastian Thrun had begun his research.

The Uber team found a handful of researchers from Carnegie Mellon in Pittsburgh that had founded a company called Carnegie Robotics. Uber quietly bought it, making it the kernel of its self-driving car team. These initial Uber employees in Pittsburgh then contacted a larger group of researchers at the National Robotics Engineering Center, part of Carnegie Mellon's Robotics Institute. In one fell swoop beginning in December 2014, Uber hired sixty researchers away from NREC, as it is known. Says Holden: "We were all very convinced that we had a chance to be the ones to usher in self-driving technology for the world."

Carnegie Mellon was stunned. Uber had gutted a key affiliate, in what seemed like an indiscriminate raid of engineers, only some of whom had any automotive experience. As word began to seep out, Uber and CMU agreed to do damage control. Uber offered to give Carnegie Mellon a gift of $5.5 million, and the two issued a statement saying that they would form a "strategic partnership." Beyond the funding for faculty positions, the "partnership" was nothing more than a recognition that Uber had created its self-driving car center with Carnegie Mellon's talent. Uber had gotten what it wanted and at minimal expense. CMU's loss, though, was the city of Pittsburgh's gain. Uber kept its researchers there and made Pittsburgh a major hub for its self-driving vehicle project.

⊙————————————————————————⊙

Over the course of 2015 and 2016, Uber's Pittsburgh arm quietly went about its work of trying to catch up with Google and a handful of other technology developers, including Tesla Motors, which had introduced driver-assistance technology in its all-electric cars. In August 2016, Uber announced its cars were ready for a limited public showing in Pittsburgh, and it invited the media for a show-and-tell session there. The cars weren't truly autonomous in that they still needed human supervision. Each had an Uber engineer behind a steering wheel should something go wrong. While the event garnered Uber global headlines for having been first to deploy self-driving taxis for commercial purposes, the scientific community was skeptical. "I think part of the reason that they released the news about these autonomous taxis is marketing," Herman Herman, NREC's director, told the online publication *Motherboard*. "Technically, I'm not sure if it's ready. They still have to have engineers in the car. So, for technical reasons, it's not there. But for non-technical reasons, they decided that it's a good idea to start talking about it."

Uber also proved itself much better at wooing local government officials than in its cease-and-desist days. After Uber debuted its cars on the streets of Pittsburgh, Mayor Bill Peduto told *The Washington Post* how Kalanick had personally pitched him, comparing Uber's "Pittsburgh Project" to the atomic-bomb-making Manhattan Project in World War II. It took a politician to raise the uncomfortable topic of what impact self-driving cars would have on drivers. "I had dinner with him one night," Peduto told the *Post*. "I asked, 'Do you know a lot of people are worried about this? About cars without humans? That it's causing people anxiety to think they are driving down the street and the car next to them won't have anybody driving?'" Kalanick and two of his engineers responded by changing the subject. "And they said, you know, people should be worried about things like genetic engineering—how DNA could be tampered with. That went into a conversation about a South Korean operation where you can clone animals." Peduto later soured on Uber, telling *The Pittsburgh Post-Gazette* in early 2017 that Uber wasn't living up to its commitments to the city. "I need to see more interest from them in our communities, both locally and internationally," he said.

Pittsburgh wasn't the only place Kalanick was looking for talent. In the summer of 2016 he had begun taking long walks in San Francisco with a former Google engineer named Anthony Levandowski, the entrepreneur whose company Google had bought and merged with its self-driving car program. Levandowski had left Google in 2016, and he started Otto, a secretive company working to apply self-driving car technology to long-haul trucking. Kalanick says his meanderings with Levandowski—they traveled on foot for miles down San Francisco's Market Street and around the famed Embarcadero all the way to the Golden Gate

Bridge—amounted to a walking tutorial on the science behind autonomy. In August 2016, Uber announced it would buy Otto for about 1 percent of Uber's value, or $680 million at the time, plus 20 percent of future profits from its trucking business. Levandowski would take over responsibility for all of Uber's self-driving efforts.

What looked to be a promising addition would prove to be another source of anxiety for Kalanick. In early 2017, Google's renamed self-driving car unit, Waymo, filed suit against Levandowski and Uber. It charged that Levandowski had downloaded thousands of files describing Google's technology before leaving the company. Uber labeled Waymo's claims "baseless."

Meanwhile, everywhere there was competition. Uber had signed a deal with Volvo to fit the Swedish manufacturer's cars with Uber's self-driving technology. Other automakers took notice. Over the course of 2016 General Motors took a major stake in Lyft and then bought Cruise Automation, a two-year-old self-driving car software company, for $1 billion. The GM investment allowed Lyft to continue competing in selected markets with Uber. It also gave GM a built-in partner with a national network so it could run experiments with its self-driving technology. Google tested a service in the Bay Area based on its Waze mapping software that let ordinary drivers connect with people looking for rides. The Google test didn't aim to make money as it asked riders only to reimburse drivers for their gasoline costs. Instead, Google was experimenting with a business model that enhanced the value of its smartphone software, Android, and also paved the way for its own eventual self-driving taxi service.

Looming largest for Uber, at least in the ultracompetitive mind of Travis Kalanick, were Tesla and its founder, Elon Musk.

Tesla had added a controversial feature to its electric cars called Autopilot, a kind of glorified cruise control that allowed drivers to take their hands off the steering wheel during highway driving. Rumors had begun to circulate that Musk coveted more than the self-driving car market. As part of a long-established goal of creating products that didn't rely on fossil fuels—Musk had started the solar panel company Solar City, which he merged with Tesla in late 2016—the Tesla founder was assumed to be exploring a ridesharing service of his own.

Kalanick had heard the rumors. When Apple, which was widely believed to be developing an electric car, invested $1 billion in Didi Chuxing, Uber's competitor in China, Kalanick called Musk to suggest the two companies find a way to work together. "I said, 'Look man, we should partner,'" Kalanick says, making the case that Apple constituted a bigger threat to Tesla than to Uber. Musk, says Kalanick, pooh-poohed the idea of a self-driving ridesharing service—and of totally autonomous cars altogether. "Elon spent the rest of the call convincing me that it's too far out and it's not realistic, that I should just stick to what we do best and be focused or I'm going to fuck it all up. That's when I knew that Tesla was competing."

It wasn't merely a hunch for Kalanick that Musk wasn't being straight with him. He says that at the same time he was talking to Musk, Uber's Jeff Holden "was talking to their head of technology, who said that driverless was" Tesla's number-one priority. Indeed, in a matter of days Musk posted online a comprehensive ten-year plan for Tesla that spelled out precisely how he planned to take on Uber. In the manifesto, which also divulged his plans for designing solar-powered roofs in Teslas and for transforming

Tesla into a high-volume producer, Musk revealed a plan for allowing Tesla owners to share their cars via a smartphone app. "You will also be able to add your car to the Tesla shared fleet just by tapping a button on the Tesla phone app and have it generate income for you while you're at work or on vacation, significantly offsetting and at times potentially exceeding the monthly loan or lease cost," Musk wrote. Then he delivered the direct shot across Uber's bow that Kalanick had been fearing: "In cities where demand exceeds the supply of customer-owned cars, Tesla will operate its own fleet, ensuring you can always hail a ride from us no matter where you are."

Uber had gotten out to a fast start and taken huge leads in markets across the United States and in many cities around the world. As the moves by the likes of GM, Google, Tesla, and others showed, however, this early lead only whetted the appetite for others to compete. But Uber continues to make surprising turns. In early 2017 it reached a nonexclusive agreement with German automaker Daimler for its autonomous vehicles to run on Uber's "platform." Daimler knew how to make the cars but had no system for arranging rides. The move began a new chapter for Uber's autonomous strategy. On the one hand it was working with Volvo to help that company develop cars with Uber technology. This put Uber in a position to sell that software to other carmakers too, a strategy that seemed to mirror Google's approach. On the other hand, its deal with Daimler focused on exploiting Uber's worldwide driver-passenger network, an asset that also could benefit other auto companies that wanted to develop their own self-driving cars but needed a way to make money off them. Uber appeared to be hedging its bets, a big-company tactic if there ever was one.

CHAPTER 11
Outflanked in China

The leaders of Uber's business in China had gathered at the sumptuous Banyan Tree resort in Hangzhou, a coastal city of some 10 million people not far from Shanghai, in the summer of 2016. They were eighteen general managers in all, each responsible for a city or a region of China. Dressed casually but sharply, the men wore fashion-forward jeans, the women colorful slacks or skirts. All were in the their thirties, give or take a half a decade, and everyone spoke outstanding English. In other words, not one of the Uber China executives would have looked out of place at Uber's headquarters in San Francisco, which each of them had visited as part of their Uber orientation.

They had come together for an important sit-down with the rather Californian CEO of their very American company. Meeting for two hours in a windowless conference room at the five-star hotel on the outskirts of town, the general managers of Uber China settled in for a no-holds-barred question-and-answer session with Travis Kalanick. On the agenda was the state of the affairs in one of Uber's most high-profile and problematic markets. They sat at four tables arranged in a square so that they could all face one another. Kalanick, at the corner of two tables farthest from the door, kicked off the meeting by requesting an around-the-horn self-introduction: name, city, and length of Uber tenure. After everyone had spoken and the floor belonged again to the CEO, he turned it right back over to the locals: "Hi. I'm Travis. I started this damn thing. I'm ready for your questions."

Uber had at this point been in China for nearly three years. And while its business there was growing, the market was also a money pit. Locked in a battle with a homegrown rival named Didi Chuxing, Uber's China unit was losing in the neighborhood of a billion dollars a year. In a legal and corporate governance maneuver it deployed only in the world's second-largest economy, the San Francisco company had established Uber China as a separate entity, headquartered in Beijing. It did so for several reasons. Mindful of the failure of other Silicon Valley companies to establish beachheads in China—Google, Facebook, and eBay were prominent and painful examples—it wanted its outpost there to be as Chinese as possible, rather than merely a subsidiary. It also didn't want the losses in China, a brutally competitive market no matter how well Uber did, to affect what was beginning to be a profitable business in the United States and other countries. Though Uber would be Uber China's largest shareholder, meaning that Uber's investors indirectly owned Uber China too, the Chinese company would have separate investors, including several from China itself.

Chosen in part for their tenacity and willingness to stand up to authority, the Chinese executives were hardly cowed by Kalanick. They quickly unleashed a barrage of questions—all with the undercurrent of trying to take the pulse of Kalanick's commitment to China. When, the locals wanted to know, would Uber China have its own engineering crew, enabling it to cease relying on software fixes from San Francisco? When would Uber China's mapping products improve? What was Kalanick's view on Chinese regulations, which Uber and Didi sometimes followed and sometimes didn't? When would Uber expand its one-city trial of UberCommute from the western metropolis of Chengdu to the rest of China? When, for that matter, would China be able to offer UberEats, the food-delivery service whose early success Kalanick had been crowing about back home? Foremost on their minds was Uber's open-warfare competition with Didi. Why, for example, was Kalanick so opposed to the idea of Uber China offering a ride-hailing app for taxi drivers, which constituted the bulk of Didi's business?

The depth and relentlessness of the questioning can easily be viewed as a good thing, a window into the healthy growing pains of a vibrant start-up, one whose able on-the-ground leaders were unafraid to challenge the visiting boss. At the same time, the topics they raised revealed the shaky state of Uber's ongoing slug-it-out contest with Didi. The angst of the executives also showed an uncomfortable truth: Uber China may legally have been an independent Chinese entity, but Travis Kalanick was calling the shots for it from San Francisco. Indeed, unable to find the right candidate to lead the country overall, Kalanick personally had been serving as Uber China's CEO—from six thousand miles and fifteen time zones away.

Kalanick, in the fifth day of a weeklong trip to China, fielded each question with the world-weariness not of a giddy entrepreneur but of a corporate veteran who'd heard it all before. Security in Uber's China offices was too porous to allow local engineering, though it was a problem he hoped to lick. "Eventually we'll have as many engineers in Beijing as in San Francisco, and they won't just work on China," he said. Mapping, he promised, was a high priority, especially so Uber could better pinpoint where to pick up passengers. Regulatory compliance was tricky in China, as it was for Uber's homegrown competition, but not overly worrisome. Chinese authorities had enforced their own laws unevenly, and so far Uber's growth hadn't been seriously hampered by it. (As an example, in 2014 the municipal government of Shanghai decreed that ridesharing was illegal during rush hour, and Uber lost most of its "supply," also known as drivers; by the following week, enforcement not having materialized, all its drivers were back on the road.) Regarding UberCommute, "we want to make it really good in Chengdu and then turn it on everywhere," he said, allowing that testing in just one city was a way to avoid too much scrutiny from Didi. And as for the food-delivery service, Kalanick simply said China wasn't ready. At a conference earlier in the week he'd been more specific and dramatic about his reluctance to launch UberEats in China: "I have a Golden Rule of China," he said. "I'm only going to lose money in one business at a time."

But it was on the subject of linking taxi drivers to riders—the foundation of Didi's business—that Kalanick dug in his heels most. And the way he explained it to his China team showed his approach to the business, how earlier efforts elsewhere in the world had framed his worldview, and, importantly, how great the challenge was for Uber in China.

For starters, Kalanick just didn't like the taxi business. Everything about Uber stood in opposition to it, most importantly what he saw as the twin pillars of taxi-industry sclerosis: fixed (low) supply of cars and set (high) prices. "What consumer is pumped for a higher-priced, lower-quality product?" he asked the group. "I don't know that consumer." Simply connecting riders with taxi drivers wasn't profitable for Uber, and he had learned this the hard way in San Francisco, where Uber continued to offer such a service. "We do ten thousand trips a week for taxis in San Francisco," he said, compared with 1.5 million for UberX and UberPool. Consumers, in other words, had spoken. "We don't want to be in that business," he says, even as his executives came back to the topic repeatedly. "It's okay if you're a new GM and you want to ask these questions. I've been doing this for six years. We have to fix airport experiences, not do taxis."

The subtext of all the questions wasn't so much about taxis as it was about Didi, which was many times bigger than Uber in China. Didi operated in more than four hundred cities throughout China and had raised some $7 billion; Uber China was in a mere sixty, and already had lost $2 billion. Its position in China, in other words, was directly analogous to Lyft's in the United States. The local managers were worried, and they wanted to gauge the CEO's staying power. Kalanick was encouraging, but his enthusiasm was conditional. "As long as our efficiency is better than Didi's I'm willing to spend more money," he said, referring to the average time drivers spent transporting passengers rather than waiting for work. "If it is dramatically worse than

Didi's then there are big question marks." Significantly, he said some of Uber's investors, who did their own research into the company's finances, were telling him Didi was "way more efficient" than Uber. "I'm going to double- and triple-check that." There was an honorable way to lose the fight, he suggested. "If they beat us by being way more efficient, it would be a silver medal for us, second place," implying that to be a profitable number two wouldn't be so bad. "We would accept that. But we have to go for the gold to get the silver."

A mere two years earlier, Uber not only wasn't out for gold medals in China, it was barely on the field of play. Kalanick's ambitions for Uber had been global almost from the start, as evidenced by the company's quick move to major cities in Europe, Latin America, Southeast Asia, and India. In the spring of 2013 Uber began scouting locations in China and by August it had conducted a "soft launch" in Shanghai, meaning it quietly turned on the service and let it spread by word of mouth. It began offering luxury cars in three cities—Shanghai, Guangzhou, and Shenzhen—in February 2014. That fall it launched its "People's Uber" service, the local equivalent of UberX, with noncommercial cars driven by nonprofessional drivers.

Everything about Uber's early activities in China was humbler than its bellicosity elsewhere in the world. As Kalanick reflected in a September 2014 interview at a start-up-oriented tech conference in San Francisco, China was a massive if untapped opportunity—and Uber was the underdog. There were two hundred cities in China with more than a million people, he noted. Two companies, one backed by Internet giant Tencent called Didi, and another by its competitor Alibaba named Kuaidi, were slugging it out against each other in an "all-out war." Both companies were paying subsidies that amounted to hundreds of millions of dollars annually. Uber, in Kalanick's perhaps wishful telling, was something of a happy-go-lucky bystander. "What's fun and awesome with what's going on in China, and for me specifically, is that we get to be the little guy there and see what happens," he said.

As far as Kalanick was concerned, Uber had a front-row seat to a Chinese grudge match. Each Chinese company attempted to thwart the other by leveraging the power of their backer. Kuaidi, for example, offered Alibaba's popular Alipay phone-based payment service as a user benefit. Didi similarly utilized Tencent's WeChat messaging service to its advantage. Yet both companies focused on the taxi market, leaving Uber unencumbered to pursue its own nontaxi ride-hailing strategy. "When you're the small guy you can do things the big guy can't," said Kalanick, nostalgically evoking his entrepreneurial sensibilities and even sounding a bit wistful, given how big Uber had become in other markets. "We're so small right now that it's not going to cost much to get into the game [in China]. Right now we're doing ridesharing and just figuring out how to make it work."

Uber would remain neither small nor cost-effective in China. And its Chinese competitors proved that they were quite capable of reading international headlines describing Uber's gains around the world. Finding common cause against Uber quickly became more important than fighting each other. In February 2015, a year after Uber formally launched its luxury service, Didi and Kuaidi merged, uniting under the former company's founder, Cheng Wei. (They chose Valentine's Day, a popular marketing event in China, to announce their merger.) Cheng, who'd risen up the ranks at Alibaba, grasped from the beginning what it would take to battle Uber. He hired as his president and chief international spokeswoman a Goldman Sachs banker named Liu Qing, known in the West as Jean Liu. A daughter of the billionaire founder of computer maker Lenovo and a fluent English speaker, Liu became Cheng's liaison with Wall Street and the Western media, two key constituencies for fighting Uber.

Despite their different heritage, nationality, and core product offerings, Didi and Uber were more alike than not. Both were run by intense entrepreneurs (Cheng, in Didi's case) who were new to the upper echelons of corporate life. Like Uber, the meaning of Didi's name was amorphous, evoking the clicking sound of a smartphone notification. (*Chuxing*, the word Cheng added after dropping the name of his merger partner, Kuaidi, means "transportation.") Like Uber, Didi noodled on fringe services that might enhance its business. An example was "Test Drive," which allowed users to request specific models of cars they might then want to buy. Like Lyft and unlike Uber, Didi allowed tipping, a driver favorite. Didi also had something of a chip on its shoulder, an emotion not foreign to Travis Kalanick. Mindful that Baidu had arisen as the leading Chinese Internet search engine not so much because it was the best but because government policy made it so difficult for Google to operate in China, Didi insisted it would win based on head-on competition, not due to provincial favoritism.

Indeed, in pitching its business Didi stressed the same advantages in China that Uber stressed in the United States: efficiency from scale, more drivers, and more services linked to a singular platform. Like Uber, Didi used its size to experiment with services from carpooling to buses. "We're playing a hurdler's game," said Liu, referring to the multiple obstacles it confronted. "China is the market we know the best," she said. "It is our homeland."

Perhaps Didi's cleverest defensive maneuver was to go on the offensive on Uber's home turf. In September 2015, it invested $100 million in Uber's main U.S. rival, Lyft. Then, two months later, it unveiled a cooperation pact with two other Uber adversaries, Ola in India and GrabTaxi in Southeast Asia. The Didi-led group quickly became known in the media as the "anti-Uber alliance," and it promised to integrate one another's platforms so users could move seamlessly from one geography to the next. (The ability to use Uber while traveling internationally was a major selling point for the U.S. market-share leader.) Didi publicly compared the effort to airline code-sharing arrangements: a convenience to their customers rather than an effort to subdue Uber. "We use the word 'partnership,' not alliance," said Jean Liu, when asked its goals. This was all well and good, but not Didi's main goal. It knew as well as Uber did that funding Lyft raised Uber's costs in the United States, sapping its energy in China. Organizing the global opposition was a fringe benefit. In Didi, Uber had met its match in terms of a start-up willing to play at scale and for the long run. As Wang Gang, a Didi investor and cofounder, would later tell *Bloomberg Businessweek*: "The purpose of them grabbing a lock of our hair and us grabbing their beard isn't really to kill the other person. Everyone is just trying to win a right to negotiate in the future."

The gamesmanship between Uber and Didi reached a fever pitch in May 2016, when Didi landed a $1 billion investment from Apple, the smartphone and computer maker with a giant business in China and endless reasons to make friends there. Apple's move stunned Kalanick. He'd met with a bevy of senior Apple executives immediately before the two companies announced their deal—and Apple had given no hint that such a body blow was coming. Meanwhile, reports of Uber's China losses emerged, suggesting that Uber had seen cash outflows of $1 billion for two years running. In his June meeting in Hangzhou, Kalanick told his China executives that Uber had two paths to victory: become more efficient than Didi or wait for Didi to run out of money. Neither scenario was looking particularly likely.

◉──◉

By the summer of 2016, China had become something of an obsession for Kalanick. As acting CEO of the China entity, he often ended his day in San Francisco in the small hours of the night, on the phone with executives in Beijing. That June, the World Economic Forum invited Kalanick to be a cochair of its so-called New Champions meeting in Tianjin, a coastal city near Beijing. The meeting sought to recognize up-and-coming corporate leaders and was informally known as the "summer Davos." The association resonated with Kalanick. Nearly a decade earlier, he'd been invited to Davos and was touched to find himself in such proximity to heads of state. "I remember trudging through the snow with the president of Kenya, which felt kind of cool," he muses. "And it was." Now, in Tianjin, he'd meet, along with a small group of business leaders, with Chinese Premier Li Keqiang, renowned for his technocratic acumen and support for entrepreneurialism.

Kalanick was an unabashed fan of China—and its political leadership. Where others saw an authoritarian regime, he saw pragmatists who allowed "the best answer to win." It was his image of how Uber operated too, the best answer winning out over emotion. Kalanick knew the unemotional facts were that Uber was losing in China, and indeed, even as he was speaking publicly about his company's ambitions and privately with local managers about its operations, his top deal maker, Emil Michael, had begun suing for peace with Didi, working out the terms of Uber's capitulation. Even still, he kept up appearances. Deals, after all, sometimes fall through. While Kalanick was traveling to Hangzhou for his meeting with his general managers, his lieutenants discussed what title to put on his business card in China. They settled on "warrior-philosopher-pioneer."

Already, though, he knew it was time to quit. On August 1, the company announced it would sell its China operations to Didi in return for a 17.7 percent stake in the Chinese company. As far as losing went, the terms were favorable to Uber. It had invested about $2 billion in China—the money it lost on operations—but would emerge with an investment in Didi worth about $6 billion. Didi would also invest $1 billion in Uber's worldwide operations, and each company would take nonvoting seats on the other's board of directors. In a blog post that read like a political concession speech, Kalanick acknowledged that China was too big a market not to have tried to conquer. "However," he wrote, in a widely quoted phrase, "as an entrepreneur, I've learned that being successful is about listening to your head as well as following your heart." For either company to be profitable Uber would have to give up, he reasoned.

And so, like the Chinese bureaucrats and politicians Kalanick so admired, he had made the pragmatic decision to take the money and concede defeat. The "silver medal," it turns out, wasn't to be a Chinese Avis to Didi's Hertz. Without the gold, Kalanick took what he saw as defeat with honor. He'd settle for a financial stake in the China market and, he hoped, a fearsome competitor no longer making mischief in his own.

CHAPTER 12

A Long Walk Through San Francisco

t is 7:30 P.M. on a sunny mid-July evening in 2016, and I've arrived at Uber's San Francisco headquarters building at this unusual hour for what has been promised to be a long interview with Travis Kalanick. I'm told he has blocked out two hours for our chat. Having a business meeting at this hour is a bit out of the norm for me, but far less so for Kalanick and his social set. In the world that doesn't revolve around start-ups and disruption and innovation, what I like to call the "real" economy, evenings are for family time or for business meals at an expense-account restaurant. But A-list San Francisco entrepreneurs are just getting warmed up around now. The coder lifestyle means late nights and late starts the next morning. For Kalanick, the end of other people's workday is a time for longer conversations, for reflection—but still for work.

I'm a bit surprised to see so few people in the office, given

Uber's penchant for long hours. It is the middle of the summer, so perhaps the young staff is out enjoying itself. But it's also possible the company's workforce is mellowing, fatigued from five-plus years of galloping at breakneck speed. Kalanick himself sets the pace. He is days from his fortieth birthday on this July night and still very much leading the young entrepreneur's Mountain Dew–fueled lifestyle. Over the years he has often had a steady girlfriend, but has remained resolutely unmarried. For the past couple years he dated a violinist and part-time tech company employee named Gabi Holzwarth, about fifteen years his junior. Multiple friends describe Kalanick as something of a homebody when not working, yet far more committed to Uber than to any other relationship. Within weeks the tabloids will reveal that Kalanick and Holzwarth have split up. She will promptly delete her many photos of Kalanick from her widely shared Facebook page.

On this night, Kalanick most definitely is working. He arrives at his desk, where I am waiting, a few minutes past the appointed hour. He has a private nook at the far end of the floor, where he keeps some clothes as well as a diorama of Uber's proposed new headquarters in the Mission Bay section of town, across the street from where the Golden State Warriors basketball team is building a new stadium. It is scheduled to open in 2018. But to the extent that Kalanick sits, which isn't much, it is at an open-plan desk at the edge of the company's fourth-floor main offices. There's nothing fancy or corner-office about it.

After a year of researching Kalanick, his past companies, and Uber, I know enough to be flexible: he likes to play it loose, to affect at least an air of spontaneity. We haven't discussed our interview agenda ahead of time other than that we'll continue the conversation about his career that we began the month before in China. He tells me he has a few things he wants to show me before we start talking, that is, if I'm willing to accept an unconventional suggestion. "Okay, you've got two choices," he announces, after greeting me. "We can go in that room," he says, pointing at a nearby conference room, one of many at Uber used for private meetings, "and I'm going to fucking pace back and forth the entire time. Or we can go for a walk."

Understanding my true choice to be between letting Travis be Travis on the one hand and trying to pry information out of a penned-in subject on the other, I opt for a walk.

Because we've grabbed our jackets—even clear July nights in San Francisco can be brisk—I assume a walk means we'll leave the building. And we will. But first Kalanick explains that he wants to give me a tour of Uber's offices. Like other hands-on CEOs before him, Kalanick views his company's offices not only as a reflection of the company's values and aspirations, but as an extension of his own personality. Steve Jobs was the same way. Six months before his death he sat down on a couch next to me in his Palo Alto living room and proudly showed me a bound book of architectural drawings for the new Apple corporate campus he wouldn't live to see. Months later he personally worked with an arborist to pick the apricot trees for the project. Kalanick, a few years younger than Jobs was when he returned to Apple for his second and final run, was communicating that to understand Uber's work space was to understand Uber itself. It was also clear that divining Uber was the key to knowing the true nature of Travis Kalanick.

"You know when, like, a city is made from scratch?" he asks. "You've got clean lines everywhere. This is like a manufactured city. So this is clean lines. We have five brand pillars: grounded, populist, inspiring, highly evolved, and elevated. That's the personality of Uber." We are standing near his desk, looking out over the nerve center of Uber's offices, the row after row of adjoining desks a visitor sees after first passing through security and entering the place where employees control Uber's global operations. As Kalanick repeats these brand "pillars"—grounded, populist, inspiring, highly evolved, and elevated—I nod my head in acknowledgment. But I never completely understand what they are all about. It's all a bit squishy, no matter how earnestly he explains them. By "grounded" he generally means practical. Uber is the ultimate in practicality: it uses technology to move people from one place to another. Yet the concept takes on new meaning in the words spoken by the son of a public-works engineer who, like many future engineers, gorged on science-fiction books as a youth. "Grounded is like tonality," says Kalanick. "It's like functional straight lines, the whole thing. All of the conference rooms are named for cities. They're in alphabetical order. Like it's just very practical."

As an example of Uber's "elevated" nature, Kalanick points to the acoustically pure ceilings in a conference room. A quiet freak himself—"I don't like sound. I don't do well with lots of noise"—he proudly identifies the building material, K-13, that pulls off the effect. "It makes it so that when you have eight hundred people on this floor, the acoustic treatment makes it calm. So I can talk softly," he says, lowering his voice to an almost awkwardly gentle murmur, "and you can hear me."

Nearby is a corridor between the desks and an interior wall. Kalanick invites me to look down into the concrete floor, where an intricate pattern is etched with a series of intersecting lines. "Right here is the San Francisco grid, stamped over and over again. I call it the path." It is here that he paces back and forth throughout the workday, often on his cell phone. "In the daytime you'll see me here," he says. "I'll do forty-five miles a week." This is more "groundedness"—literally the connection to the ground, but also representing the grind-it-out work it takes to oversee Uber. But the homage to Uber's home city is also "elevated," a symbol of Uber's lofty aspiration to improve the quality of life in cities.

I had read of Kalanick's willingness to devote untold hours to seemingly superficial minutiae. He devoted hours, for example, to explaining to *Wired* magazine the months he spent personally overseeing the redesign of Uber's logo at a time when the company was beset by myriad seemingly more pressing crises. Yet I hadn't personally witnessed his willingness to dive into the weeds—nor how committed he was to seemingly arcane and ethereal aspects of such a demanding business.

The tour proceeds around the fourth floor. Kalanick shows me "New York City," the conference room where Uber negotiated the deal in which it raised $1.2 billion, just before the company moved into the Market Street offices. "The first billion-dollar deal that blew people's minds," he exclaims proudly. We take an elevator to the eleventh floor, where Kalanick has created an austere setting, a place to mimic the entrepreneurial environment, with exposed drywall and smaller-than-usual desks. "When you're an entrepreneur, at least the ninety-nine percent of entrepreneurs that are not Mark Zuckerberg, you have hard times," he says. "So this right here is what I call the cave, because when you're going through hard times you're in the dark, you're literally in some dark place. It's a metaphor." I ask if the desks, which Kalanick proudly tells me are "tighter by a foot," are a nod to Jeff Bezos, who long decreed that desks at Amazon be made of doors, a common practice in the giant's early days. Kalanick's response: "Not even that. It's just my nod to myself. Like how I experienced being an entrepreneur."

Down on the fifth floor are areas with conference rooms named after science-fiction books. Kalanick knows the sci-fi canon the way a Civil War buff rattles off important battles. One section is named for Isaac Asimov's Foundation series, another for *The Martian*, a third for *Ender's Game*. Explains Kalanick: "It's a book about a kid who is trained by the military to play video games, but really complex video games. But he realizes at the end that the video games he was playing were an actual war." He brands the sci-fi theme highly evolved, by which he means the future. Uber is a company obsessed with the future. Elsewhere there's a central area meant to evoke an Italian piazza. The hallways leading to it are confusing, by design. In Kalanick's worldview, disorientation is good. "So if you are a resident you know where everything is," he says. This is his version of populism. "If you are a guest you're lost. So you can tell who's a resident and who's a guest." We never overtly discuss the "inspiring" brand pillar. Presumably for Kalanick everything about his bespoke and profoundly odd headquarters office is inspiring. I never quite figure out how K-13 ceilings, video game wars, and Italian piazzas fit together at Uber. But perhaps some things aren't meant to be understood.

We leave the building by slipping past Kalanick's desk to his secret exit and staircase that lead directly out onto a street around the corner from the entrance to Uber's office. The plan, he tells me, is to walk down Market Street, the main thorough-fare that cuts through the center of downtown San Francisco, to the Embarcadero along the waterfront. From there we'll head to the touristy Fisherman's Wharf area and toward the Golden Gate Bridge. Despite the brilliant sunset, the temperature is falling. Kalanick, forever an Angeleno, can't bear it. "This is the most upsetting thing for somebody from Los Angeles," he says. "That's why I sometimes do weekends in LA. Just to be at the beach."

Kalanick is in a reflective mood, and as we walk he riffs on all manner of things. I remark, for example, on how little I've heard of late about Square, the payments company headed by Twitter founder Jack Dorsey, whose offices are in the same building as Uber. Although Uber is private and Square is publicly traded, Square has become decidedly low profile. Muses Kalanick: "We don't really have that luxury." We begin talking about Kalanick's entrepreneurial history, including his desperate hunt for funding at Red Swoosh. As we make our way down the sometimes seedy, always bustling Market Street, Kalanick comments on an old Red Swoosh office and a diner where his tiny engineering team would often meet. A fire engine, sirens blaring, roars by. Kalanick keeps talking.

By the time we hit the Embarcadero, the curvilinear street that runs along the waterfront between the Bay Bridge and the Golden Gate Bridge, dusk has set in. On our narrative journey, Kalanick has arrived at the early days of Uber and is now describing its quaintly small funding rounds. I wonder aloud if he'll be recognized during our walk. Not likely, he says, so long as we're in conversation and outdoors. We discuss in great detail how Kalanick oversaw later fund-raising for Uber, including the rounds that got the company to its eventual private-market valuation of nearly $70 billion.

When we travel all the way past Fisherman's Wharf, dodging midsummer tourists from around the world, we step into an In-N-Out Burger, the greasy fast-food chain from Southern California and a Kalanick favorite. By now we are discussing driverless cars, and Kalanick suggests big moves are ahead that he can't yet discuss. He lets on that this six-mile walk, always including the In-N-Out Burger stop, has become a summer-evening routine and that he typically walks it with one person he won't identify. I later learn his walking partner is Anthony Levandowski, the ex-Google autonomous vehicles engineer who went on to found Otto, the self-driving truck company. Uber will purchase Otto just a few weeks after our walk, and Kalanick tells me he used his time with Levandowski to absorb the technology and business-plan vision for autonomous vehicles.

Having spent so much time discussing Kalanick's entrepreneurial days, I want to know how he views the bigger, more established company Uber has become. His answers betray a reluctance to think of the company that way. He doesn't know everyone at the company anymore, but he still conducts hours-long interviews with top prospects, something he did when the company was smaller. Kalanick explains that he likes to simulate what it would be like to work with someone before hiring them. I ask if he likes running a big company. "The way I do it, it doesn't feel big," he says, falling back on a favorite trope: that he approaches his day as a series of problems to be solved. He obviously thinks of himself as troubleshooter in chief as much as a CEO.

Bigness clearly is scary, though, especially for an entrepreneur who never graduated to that stage before. "I would say you constantly want to make your company feel small," he says. "You need to create mechanisms and cultural values so that you feel as small as possible. That's how you stay innovative and fast. But how you do that at different sizes is different. Like when you're super small, you go fast by just tribal knowledge. But if you did tribal knowledge when you're super big it would be chaotic and you'd actually go really slow. So you have to constantly find that line between order and chaos."

I ask if he's thought about how to make the transition that all maturing companies go through when the company is no longer comprised of a bunch of young, single people with nothing in their lives but work. "I call it the red line," he says. "In a car, you can go fast. But you have a red line. And everybody has their own personal red line. You want to push into that red line and see what that engine's made of. You might find you've got more in the tank than you thought, or more under the hood than you thought. But you can't sit over the red line for too long. And everybody's got their own personal red line." He points out that already there are many "Uber babies" and that parents tend to be more efficient than childless people with fewer constraints on their time. There are limits, though, to Kalanick's aspirations for work-life balance for his employees. "Look, if somebody's producing more, they're going to rise faster. That just is. There's no way around that."

◉───◉

After more than three hours of walking, the night has turned cold and dark. I suddenly remember that while we are talking Donald Trump is accepting his party's nomination at the Republican National Convention in Cleveland. As Kalanick and I are going over Uber's past, present, and future, Trump is telling a national audience that "I alone can fix it." The nation might be glued to their TV sets that night, but politics doesn't come up once in our conversation.

Somewhere near the Marina Green, a stretch of land next to the bay where San Francisco's first airfield was built in 1920, the conversation turns deeply personal. We discuss how Kalanick and Uber are perceived by the outside world. In one of our first meetings to discuss this book, he brought up, unsolicited, the issue of the e-mail he'd written me two years earlier, threatening to make things difficult for me if I proceeded without his cooperation. Now we turn to the narrative arc of how Uber progressed from media darling to media villain. Kalanick was an almost willing accomplice in this metamorphosis, often managing to stoke the fire by playing the villain himself. Kalanick refers to this as his "little moments of arrogance where I say something provocative," like his e-mail to me or mentioning taxi drivers and assholes in the same breath. I ask if he cares what people think. "Yeah, it's not good for Uber, it's not good for me, it's not good for the people that I'm talking to. It's bad for everybody."

Kalanick isn't able to hide his defensiveness or his annoyance. He ascribes his moments of pique to "fierce truth seeking." Someone willing to say exactly what he thinks, empathy be damned, will be judged harshly. He's not alone. It's a trait that's been repeatedly ascribed to Steve Jobs, Jeff Bezos, and to Kalanick's contemporary Elon Musk. Kalanick is aware of this, referring to the "meme that founder-CEOs have to be assholes to be successful." He rejects that notion, but he's obviously just short of obsessed by it. "I think there's this question out there," he says, shifting away from general memes to himself. "Is he an asshole? Since you've spent time with me, one of the big questions you're going to get is, is he an asshole?"

Engineer that he is, Kalanick wants to believe there is a scientific answer to the question. I suggest the answer is and always will be in the realm of opinion, not fact. He rejects this. "Understanding whether it's real or not, like do I trigger something in certain people that's related to something that I didn't do? Or am I an asshole? I'd love to know." He continues: "I don't think I'm an asshole. I'm pretty sure I'm not." But I want to know if he cares one way or the other what people think. "What you're hearing me say is that if you are a truth seeker, you just want the truth. And if you believe that something is not the truth, then you want to keep seeking for truth. That's just how I'm wired."

Kalanick is unlikely to ever hear the version of the truth he craves. Weeks after our walk, *New York* magazine publishes an interview with Bradley Tusk, the political consultant who has worked for Uber on multiple regulatory fights. In discussing his own willingness to take "a few hits" for the right reasons, Tusk compares himself to Kalanick. "He understands to achieve really big things, you're going to piss a lot of people off," Tusk says. Then the *New York* writer asks Tusk if Kalanick is an asshole and describes his reaction. "He hesitates. 'Are we off the record?' I tell him we are not. 'No, he is not an asshole.'" Of course, the question would be answered for good in early 2017 when a video of Kalanick berating a driver went viral. Kalanick suggested publicly the incident showed his need to "grow up." But he said this having recently entered his fifth decade. Youthfulness simply couldn't explain his behavior.

Kalanick, who at this point in our walk is cold and tired, offers to continue to the Golden Gate Bridge, likely another half hour down the trail, or to call a car and head back to the Uber offices. I'm tired and cold too, but I ask him to choose. "I think we're getting a car," he says.

⊙————————————————————————⊙

He pulls out his smartphone and summons an Uber. It takes the driver just a few minutes of listening to our discussion to realize that the "Travis" he has picked up—all Uber drivers have the first name of their paying passenger—is the company's CEO.

DRIVER: Are you Travis?

KALANICK: Yeah. How you doing, man?

DRIVER: I never met you.

KALANICK: Yeah, yeah.

DRIVER: How you doing, man?

KALANICK: I'm good, I'm good.

DRIVER: I can't believe it.

KALANICK: How'd you connect the dots? You were chilling there for a little bit.

DRIVER: I was looking in the rearview mirror a little bit. And you looked so familiar. Damn, I'm with the CEO.

KALANICK: It's good to meet you, man.

DRIVER: Thanks, man.

KALANICK: How long you been doing the Uber thing?

DRIVER: A year, about a year and two months.

KALANICK: What were you doing before?

DRIVER: I was doing it part time because I live in San Francisco, so I need more money.

KALANICK: For sure.

DRIVER: And then I got laid off, so I'm doing it full time now.

The conversation that ensues begins the casual way so many driver-to-passenger chats do in Ubers and taxis. Then it takes a unique turn. The driver explains that he'd recently been laid off after sixteen years at AT&T, where he worked in tech support.

Kalanick asks if he is "pumped" about being able to control his time now as an Uber driver, and the driver says he likes the flexibility, though the money could be better. When Kalanick tries suggesting the company has lots of ways for people like the driver "to make an extra buck," the tide turns. "Well, your tech support really sucks," the driver says. "That's true, I'm working on it," says Kalanick, asking for a few months to fix what's broken.

But realizing his captive audience, the driver has more to say. Much more. A laid-off tech-support man himself, he wants to know if Uber's tech support is overseas. "Some of them are," Kalanick replies. "But it's not even about that. I mean it's partially the story. But the bottom line is I apologize, and it will get better soon." The driver also complains that he's not getting e-mails and text messages informing him of guaranteed hours, an incentive program that is a staple for drivers trying to make a living on Uber. Kalanick promises to send an e-mail from the backseat, which pleases the driver immensely. "Cool. Because I write to them and they don't speak English. They don't know what I'm talking about. I almost wrote a book, because I have pages and pages." The driver then gives the CEO a lesson on how drivers abuse Uber's rules. For example, many drivers screen rides to avoid undesirable destinations, like far-out suburbs. The two have an unproductive back-and-forth with Kalanick arguing that surge pricing outside of San Francisco means drivers can make good money and the driver insisting the pay doesn't justify the hassle.

By the time we get out of the car, near 11:00 P.M., Kalanick has promised to follow up. (At 11:07 P.M. he forwards me an internal response from a "senior community operations manager" in Chicago promising to look into the driver's problems. I ask months later if he would have been as responsive if I hadn't been in the car. "You know how many e-mails and texts I send from cars, from drivers giving me feedback?" he asks. "Uber product managers are like, 'Oh man, here we go.'" This was before the video surfaced of his less than cordial exchange with another driver.) We get out at the same side entrance where we exited the Uber building hours earlier. The car doesn't linger. As we are opening our doors the driver receives his next pickup request nearby, and he speeds off to find his passenger.

***

As 2016 drew to an end, Uber's future began to come into focus. But just barely. Giving up on China was a significant step forward in terms of cleaning up a financial mess that showed no end in sight. Uber's financial well-being leaked in dribs and drabs, revealing a mixed and incomplete picture. The company lost $800 million in the third quarter of the year, but was on track to record nearly $6 billion in net revenues for the entire year. Observers and the company's own investors weren't sure how to analyze the numbers and Uber's prospects for profitability. That's because driver subsidies, passenger sign-up bonuses, and R&D investment costs obscured what kind of business Uber ultimately could be. Competitors promised to be a continued thorn in Uber's side too. Lyft, flush with GM's investment, continued to lose as much as $50 million a month. In early 2017 it vowed to expand into an additional one hundred U.S. cities. Juno, the ridesharing company that bragged about taking a smaller cut from its drivers, threatened to expand beyond New York.

Kalanick had little trouble recruiting top talent. Keeping them was another matter. In the fall he hired a new president for ridesharing operations, a Target marketing executive named Jeff Jones. Once again, Ryan Graves stepped back from a job to make way for a newcomer. Jones would only last six months. Kalanick also added some star power to Uber's board, recruiting publisher and author Arianna Huffington as a director. Kalanick would credit Huffington with advancing his emotional intelligence as an entrepreneur and executive. Then, early in 2017, Uber hired a former top Google search engineer, Amit Singhal, as senior vice president of engineering. Kalanick crowed about the importance of the hire. Yet Singhal left Uber weeks later after word surfaced that he'd left Google amid allegations of sexual harassment and failed to inform Uber of this. (Singhal denied having harassed anyone.) Days after Singhal's departure, growth chief Ed Baker resigned without explanation. Then, Jeff Jones resigned after Kalanick announced that he'd hire a chief operating officer, calling into question Jones's role at the company.

Despite its size, Uber continued to behave like a start-up at least in terms of the flexibility of its business practices. In early 2016 *The New York Times* reported that an Uber executive vowed the company would never provide for tipping. Mere months later Uber walked back that vow by allowing drivers to post signs that solicited tips. The company promised never to abandon surge pricing, no matter how much it enraged riders. Yet in mid-2016 it moved toward a system of informing riders up front what the price of their trip would be. This simultaneously maintained a method of dynamic pricing while no longer rubbing it in a customer's face that they were paying so many times the normal rate.

Uber also showed it hadn't lost the appetite to dream big. In late October 2016, its top product executive, Jeff Holden, published a ninety-nine-page white paper devoted to Uber's research into flying cars, of all things. He dubbed the project "Uber Elevate." The report begins: "Imagine traveling from San Francisco's Marina to work in downtown San Jose—a drive that would normally occupy the better part of two hours—in only 15 minutes." It goes on to explain Uber's vision for a network of cars that take off and land vertically and the infrastructure it would take to build it. The paper might have seemed like an April Fool's joke closer to Halloween, but for its detailed discussion of "market feasibility barriers" and its seventeen-person contributor-and-reviewer roster, including scientists from NASA, Georgia Tech, and MIT. One of those reviewers, a thirty-year NASA veteran named Mark Moore, joined Uber full time in early 2017 as director of aviation engineering. Whatever Uber's shortcomings, it's safe to say it literally considers the sky to be the limit.

In the summer of 2016 I traveled by private jet with Kalanick and several top Uber executives from Beijing, the Chinese capital, to Hangzhou, the coastal city near Shanghai that is home to Alibaba and thus an important hub of the Chinese Internet business. Kalanick was on his way to meet with his top managers in China, and also to attend a conference hosted by Jack Ma, Alibaba's charismatic CEO. It was during this downtime that Kalanick was at his most relaxed. In the hangar waiting for takeoff, Kalanick muses about how rarely Uber pays to fly private. (This plane had been hired for a trip to Korea—when Kalanick was going to appear in court there—that got called off.) Talk of private jets led to a reminiscence about the annual media conference in Sun Valley, Idaho, hosted by the investment bank Allen & Co., which is popular with media moguls with their own planes. Kalanick has been only once and was miffed he hadn't been invited back, which surprises me. We've just come from a World Economic Forum event he cochaired and where he met the Chinese premier, yet he is focused on his missing invitation from Allen & Co. He jokes that he'd like to program a welcome message from him for Allen & Co. attendees who request cars from Uber: "We hope you have a good Uber experience this week . . . please tell the Allen & Co. people to invite me."

For all his professed just-the-facts practicality, Kalanick loves nothing more than to bat around ideas, the zanier the better. He wonders aloud to Emil Michael, his top deal maker and fund-raiser, if Uber could go public without investment bankers. Michael, a lawyer by training, suggests instead a reverse merger, a somewhat dubious technique whereby a private company buys an inferior public company for its listing. Kalanick suggests using no bankers but giving 3 percent of the capital raised—the fee bankers would have received—to charity. When I suggest giving that money instead to drivers, Kalanick lights up. He says he wants to give equity to drivers, something upstart Juno has begun doing, but Uber has found the securities-law implications to be complicated.

Once airborne, Kalanick turns positively pensive. He tells me he has long dreamed of being an investigative journalist, having once read an anthology of reporting about the Khmer Rouge in Cambodia. The "dream job," he says, appeals to his sense of justice. He even has an idea for an investigative project: he and I need to go to Mumbai for six months, he says, and live in the slums and write about the experience. "I'm going to grow out my hair and wear different clothes and go native," he says. (I suggest my family life might make this project difficult. "Then we'll wait until your daughter is older," he says.)

I learn over time that this is partly how Kalanick amuses himself and partly a reflection of his earnest side. He's a seeker, a dreamer. If he's moved by the plight of the Cambodian people under the murderous Khmer Rouge or by the slum dwellers of Mumbai, he hasn't done anything about the homeless in his own city of San Francisco. His ideas are thrilling but also baffling, and he relishes challenges to his flights of fancy. I'm reminded of his pitch to me for a new kind of media company, in which companies commission journalists to write stories while reserving full veto power. We argued vehemently about it. I told him all the reasons it wouldn't work, and he stubbornly insisted it could be a valid business model. Neither of us made any headway with the other, and we are each unperturbed by the argument.

Everyone has an opinion on Uber, much the way five years ago everyone had an opinion about Apple. As I was finishing the manuscript for this book, a friend cornered me at a party because he wanted to tell me about his recent Uber experience. He lives in an outer suburb of Marin County, north of San Francisco and a relatively undesirable trip for Uber drivers. On the one hand, it's a good fare to go all that way, more than thirty miles. Yet drivers would routinely turn him down when he plugged his suburban town into the "destination" field on the Uber app—in violation of their compact with Uber. The problem is that they were nearly certain to return to San Francisco empty. Moreover, Uber's incentives favor volume of trips over mileage. A long haul to northern Marin would count as one ride and might kill an hour.

On my friend's recent trip, he was returning late at night from the East Coast and flew into San Francisco International Airport. After several rejections, the driver who accepted him was a "crazy Russian" who carried on an argumentative banter from the front seat and persisted in weaving through traffic at high speeds. My friend gamely suggested that living to see his children was more important to him than getting home quickly, and when the driver repeatedly ignored his pleas he asked to be let off at the side of the road, just over the Golden Gate Bridge but still many miles from home. He complained to Uber about the driver's behavior and a couple hours later was pleasantly surprised to receive a sympathetic response. But for the time being, he was in a quandary. He was at the side of a road, not exactly sure where he was. It was late at night. He wanted to go home. So what did he do? He requested an Uber to come pick him up. "That's where they've come to in the zeitgeist: I was furious with Uber, but utterly dependent on Uber as the only reasonable alternative to hailing a driver that would have the ability to find me."

⊙───⊙

Where you stand on Uber more often than not is a product of where you sit. In early 2016, when a group of New York City drivers, a polyglot of outer-borough-dwelling immigrants who had formed the core of Uber's workforce, protested their perceived shabby treatment by Uber, *The New York Times* made a trenchant observation about Kalanick's tactlessness. "Uber has been somewhat clumsy in dealing with the problems with its fleet," the *Times* wrote. "In a stroke of unfortunate timing, *Wired* magazine published a 3,000-word treatise on Uber's new corporate logo one day after the drivers went on strike outside its New York City office. It was an inadvertent study in tech-world navel-gazing: as hundreds of immigrants were splashed across the Internet attacking Uber, *Wired* describes how Mr. Kalanick had been working for two years on the logo, immersing himself in organic color schemes and kerning."

The fact is, these are precisely the matters that engross Kalanick and his fellow entrepreneurs. He may have spent the bulk of his twenties and into his thirties with his nose pressed up against the glass, desperately seeking to get inside. But the place he sought entry into is an unreal world, as removed as one can be from the pedestrian life of Uzbek hacks in Queens.

Indeed, though Kalanick blanches at acknowledging any influences, obsessing over the "kerning" of a logo is exactly what Steve Jobs did at Apple. And he was revered for it. Kalanick never met Jobs, but everyone in Silicon Valley can recite the lines from the hymnal of how Jobs wouldn't rest until every font, typeface, and finely beveled edge had reached perfection. The Apple CEO was a master at instilling cognitive dissonance, persuading customers to overlook (usually fixable) defects in his products as well as the troubling working conditions of the contractors who made them. Similarly, Amazon's Jeff Bezos gets away with jerking around just about everyone—suppliers, employees, shippers, other merchants—so long as he delivers the lowest prices to customers.

So far, Kalanick has succeeded neither at creating the type of "reality-distortion field" for which Jobs was famous nor at convincing the lion's share of Uber's riders and drivers to overlook his callous statements and outward lack of empathy for their plight. He has been troubled enough at how he and his company are perceived to try to do something about it: devoting more resources to keeping riders happy, trying to fix a badly broken customer- and driver-support infrastructure, attempting to tone down incendiary comments on the advice of highly paid image consultants.

Yet for all the external criticism and internal soul-searching, it has stopped neither the Uber juggernaut nor the constant news cycle of hubbub that surrounds it. Over and over the company finds itself at the center of controversy, often a victim of its dodgy reputation and unable to overcome it. In the first days of the new U.S. administration of Donald Trump in 2017, for example, taxi drivers in New York organized a one-hour strike at John F. Kennedy International Airport to express solidarity with immigrants detained under a travel ban hastily decreed by the White House. Uber declared, by Twitter, that it would suspend surge pricing from JFK. It too intended to help, hoping to lessen the pain of congestion around the airport due to protests against the White House policy. Critics interpreted the move as countering the taxi boycott, however, and a #DeleteUber meme spread on social media.

What looked like yet another social-media hullabaloo turned into a significant business fiasco. Not only was Uber under fire for appearing less than sympathetic to immigrant taxi drivers—already under siege by Uber itself—but drivers, riders, and Uber's own employees turned their fire on Kalanick. He, after all, had agreed to serve with seventeen other business executives on an advisory council to the president. In a statement on Facebook posted before the fateful JFK tweet from Uber's New York office, Kalanick promised to raise his opposition to the travel ban in an upcoming meeting with the president. Then the situation got out of control. Overnight, anti-Uber fury spread on social media. The next morning, January 29, 2017, Lyft fanned the flames by announcing a $1 million donation to the American Civil Liberties Union over four years. Later that day, Uber pledged to create a $3 million defense fund for immigrant drivers affected by the ban, a move that appeared to be in reaction to Lyft. But the damage had been done. More than 200,000 users deleted their Uber accounts, and in an all-hands meeting that week Uber employees told Kalanick directly how upset they were with his involvement with the president. Kalanick, famous for his stubbornness, resigned from Trump's advisory council on February 2, a second shockingly pragmatic move just months after capitulating to Didi in China.

Pragmatic or not, and fair or not, Uber suffered the consequences of its reputation—and Kalanick's—that it couldn't shake. And the consequences were real, even if the durability of the defections would remain tough to measure. Indeed, Kalanick would remain an enigma whose reputation inside the company was quite different than outside. Employees laud him for taking feedback from the lowliest intern. Many believe it was the anguish of employees—not the sting of lost business—that caused him to ditch his position on the Trump council. And yet the hits kept coming. Just as the #DeleteUber storm abated, the allegations of ignored complaints of sexual harassment from a female engineer became the next social-media storm to engulf Uber.

For all the controversies and its constant stay in the spotlight, then, Uber is like nothing that came before it. At just a few years of age it has already changed consumer behavior around the world. It excited, then alienated, and then more or less satisfied legions of customers and drivers. It took advantage of widely available technology, showing the way for untold other entrepreneurial upstarts to try something similar. And yet its future is complicated. It is admired, but less frequently loved. It has market power, but many enemies who rejoice at every Uber setback. It is boldly investing in the future, knowing full well the risks that its advantages of venture-capital wealth and market leadership might not be enough to counter a cleverer or richer adversary.

In one of my last conversations with Kalanick, I brought up the topic of Alexander Hamilton, in part to verify my recollection that Kalanick had been interested in the first U.S. treasury secretary long before Lin-Manuel Miranda's epically successful musical exploded on Broadway. Why, I asked, did Kalanick admire Hamilton so much when he first read Ron Chernow's biography? "There's much to admire about him," he said. "He was an entrepreneur in his own time. But instead of creating a company he was creating a country. He was right at the center. The U.S. would be a very different place if he wasn't there. He was a philosopher, but he was also an execution guy. He had a lot of great qualities. I think just so much about how he saw the future. And in many ways America lived that out, and I think we became a prominent country because of his vision." Hamilton didn't know when to keep quiet, and his list of enemies was long. Did Kalanick identify, I wondered, with the extraordinary amount of public abuse Hamilton withstood? "Well, look," he said. "This guy had a lot of adversity. We have this thing at Uber. We like to say, 'Know what's right, fight for it, don't be a jerk.' He just did what he thought was right. And when you do that, when you're doing something really, really different, you're going to have some naysayers. You just have to get used to that." Travis Kalanick, the philosopher/execution guy, a jerk to many but not to himself, very likely will never get used to the naysayers. Adversity, after all, had become part of the journey.

Acknowledgments

John Brodie, the editor of my first book and a friend and mentor like no other, handed me the idea for this book all but wrapped up in a bow. My literary agent, Esmond Harmsworth, is my rock, my defender, and my shoulder to cry on.

At *Fortune*, where quality journalism still matters, my friends and colleagues (past and present) are like family. My dearest *Fortune* sisters and brothers are Clifton Leaf, Stephanie Mehta, Brian O'Keefe, Jennifer Reingold, and Nick Varchaver, and I value and admire the hard work of all my colleagues. Peerless researcher Doris Burke was there for me, again, when I needed her. Ryan Derousseau buttressed my reporting in a pinch. Andy Serwer and Alan Murray, my two most recent bosses, encouraged my various adventures and tolerated my periodic absences. I also am blessed to count as members of my kitchen cabinet other giants of the Time Inc. firmament: John Huey, Rik Kirkland, Norman Pearlstine, and Walter Isaacson.

Despite the name on the spine, books are a team effort, and

my teammates at Penguin Portfolio—Natalie Horbachevsky, Stephanie Frerich, and Merry Sun—are publishing's elite athletes. I'm also grateful for the tremendous support of their colleagues Adrian Zackheim, Will Weisser, Taylor Fleming, and Katherine Valentino. Companies tend not to see a lot of upside from books about them, and Uber was no different. Nevertheless, Natasha Osborne-Guerts, Jill Hazelbaker, and Matt Kallman generously gave me time they didn't really have to give.

So many friends, not all of whom are journalists, listened, supported, and advised me over the last year. These include Chuck Coustan, Krista Donaldson, Miguel Helft, Michael Newman, John Needham, Jennifer Newton, and Jeffrey O'Brien. If the FAMRI Library at the UCSF Mission Bay campus didn't exist, I would have been forced to find somewhere else to write this book. I appreciate the kind staff there for maintaining such a peaceful oasis.

Families of authors know better than anyone the downsides of writing a book: the nights away from home, the lost weekend afternoons, the author's unbearable crankiness. My wife, Ruth Kirschner, helps me live a balanced life and puts up with my crankiness. My ten-year-old daughter Leah showed great interest in this project from start to finish. She still seems to enjoy it when I read to her at night—so long as the topic isn't business. My sisters, Paula and Amy Lashinsky, my brother-in-law, Robert Lopez, and my dad, Bernard, all gave me just the right combination of support and leeway. Finally, I wouldn't be a writer at all if my mother, Marcia Morris Lashinsky, hadn't imbued in me her love of words and her insatiable curiosity. She would have taken Ubers all over the place and then given me a detailed account of every trip. I wish she were here to read this book.